SARAH'S DIARY

SARAH'S DIARY

Sarah Griffin

This paperback edition first published in Great Britain in
2007 by
Virgin Books Ltd
Thames Wharf Studios
Rainville Road
London
W6 9HA

A catalogue record for this book is available from
the British Library.

ISBN 978 0 7535 1270 8

Typeset by TW Typesetting, Plymouth, Devon

Penguin Random House is committed to a sustainable future for
our business, our readers and our planet. This book is made from
Forest Stewardship Council® certified paper.

Printed and bound in Great Britain by Clays Ltd, Elcograf S.p.A.

For Dad

ACKNOWLEDGEMENTS

The support of my sisters – Kathryn, Emma and Rachel – is, and always has been, invaluable. Their bravery and unfaltering confidence in me has really kept this whole process going. Without them this book would still be trapped in the pages of a battered notebook. I'm endlessly grateful also to my extended family: Rich, Richard, Chris and Nick, Emma, and the other friends of various ages who have offered advice and encouragement along the way. I could not have completed this journey without the faith of Virgin and the kindness of everyone at HHB Agency. I thank them for taking that huge leap and believing in me. I also want to say a special thanks to my mum, whose strength continues to amaze me every day. Without her infinite support and continued love I would not be the person I am today.

PROLOGUE

I suppose you could say it all began in the early 1960s. The precise moment is, I've heard, difficult to pinpoint. Mum reckons it was when she was about six years old.

OK, I'll set the scene. Rivington County Primary School playground, St Helens, Merseyside. A little girl called Carol Cook falls on the hard, sloping playground. Flying through the air, she lands on both knees, and begins to cry as blood pours out of the left one. Looking up, she sees, coming over to help, a boy she recognises as the clever one in her class. His name is Robert Griffin. It's hard for me to imagine him without bushy eyebrows and a dark-brown moustache, but I guess he would have looked a bit daft with those features at the age of six.

My mum and dad were only classmates at that point, rivals for both the top spot in Maths and the favour of Mrs Hunter, their first teacher. Mum was popular; Dad was quiet and a bit of a loner. Yet maybe the six-year-old Robert saw something he liked in the impish face of young Carol because his appearances in her life became more frequent after that point, even when they went to different secondary schools at the age of eleven. He used to visit her house on the pretext of collecting newspapers for recycling, and even though the door was slammed in his face a fair few times it didn't put him off. On his sixteenth birthday, although the room was full of invited guests, when the time came for Mum to leave, he turned on all the lights and asked everyone to go so he could walk her home. Their first official date was organised by Dad's mum, Norah (Gran to me); a trip to the local cinema to see *Please, Sir.* (Funny how courtship's changed over the years; I'd be mortified if Mum did that for me now!) They used to go to the local youth club and play table tennis, where the other kids would tease them by singing Donny Osmond's 'Puppy Love'.

It sounds like a perfect seventies' teenage romance, and I'm sure it was, but it didn't stay perfect for long. Things changed when they went to different universities: Dad to Lancaster to read Accounting and Finance; Mum to York, where she read Maths and Education. After a while, Mum started getting itchy feet. In the Easter of her first year she started seeing somebody else and told Dad it was over between them. The effects were disastrous.

Devastated, Dad refused to leave his bedroom for three days. Gran began to leave his meals outside his room. It was definitely a sign of things to come. Maybe Mum shouldn't have changed her mind. Yet change her mind she did, and she wrote him a letter apologising and asking him to meet her to sort things out. I think at that point Dad realised what he could lose. He proposed shortly before Mum's twenty-first birthday. (He was traditional and asked her dad for permission first.) On 15 July 1978, two years after graduating, they were married in the same United Reformed church where they had attended youth club a few years before.

But this childhood romance was flawed. Mum began to notice things weren't quite right with her new husband, though there had been warning signs at university. Even when he passed all his accountancy exams in his final year, for example, the black cloud of exam stress hadn't lifted. But now, when things seemed so perfect for her, why wasn't he happy?

The big wake-up call came in 1980 when she got a phone call to say Dad had been knocked down in Leeds city centre by a bus. What was more, it was believed that he had walked in front of the bus intentionally. He suffered a serious head injury and had to be treated in hospital where they wanted him to receive psychiatric treatment. He refused.

Later on that year Dad took an overdose of sleeping tablets. Mum decided something had to happen. They talked about making a change (a conversation that was to be repeated many times in the years that followed) and decided to move abroad.

From 1981 to 1985 they lived in the Cayman Islands. Dad worked for a large accountancy firm and Mum taught at the island's middle school. They moved several times but lived mostly in apartments, including one that overlooked Seven Mile Beach, the infamous tourist spot. It was an area so beautiful it couldn't fail to make even the most melancholy of people crack a smile. Yet still Dad couldn't force himself to be happy. In 1982 came the birth of their first child, my eldest sister, Kathryn Jane. But walking along the golden sands of Seven Mile Beach with his newborn daughter in his arms, Dad still wasn't content. This wasn't just about materialistic happiness, Mum realised; there was something more to it. Two more daughters came: Emma Louise and Rachel Lynn. Yet still no improvement. The doctors in the Caribbean were made to feel inadequate by Dad, and they knew he needed help that they could not give him.

Persuaded by Mum, the young family moved back to the UK and settled in Huddersfield in the summer of 1985, just weeks after Rachel's birth. Another blue period soon came, however, and this time Mum sought out the help of a new young doctor, Dr Oakes, who became convinced Dad had what was known as depression. He referred them to a psychiatrist at a specialist local hospital called St Luke's. There he was told he had to be admitted for a minimum of three weeks so they could 'sort him out'. Admitted he was, and Mum, in her early thirties, with three kids under the age of three, supported him. Every day she tried to go and see him, and listened while he spouted lines of rubbish, sent manic by the 'liquid cosh' that was supposed to give the doctors a 'clean slate' on which to work. Three weeks later he came out of hospital. Mum was expecting a changed man, an instant cure almost, but the results didn't last. There were simply good days and bad.

But things did improve enough for the good to outweigh the bad (at least I like to think so) and their love for each other was still great enough to produce a fourth and final child – me. I came into this world just after 2 p.m. on Thursday, 17 December 1987 at Beverley Westwood Hospital. Dad brought my three sisters in to visit me: Kathryn aged five, Emma three and Rachel two. The sight of them made Mum realise Dad couldn't live without her. None of their clothes matched and Rachel was even wearing her winter boots on the wrong feet.

I moved into our comfortable townhouse in Beverley just days later for my first Griffin family Christmas.

Throughout my childhood, I always thought I was pretty normal, just an average child with an average family. I went to Brownies, to swimming club. We went on holiday, we visited friends. Mum and Dad had dinner parties. It was ordinary. Even though I knew there was stuff going on at home, and that Mum and Dad often had arguments and long, complicated discussions, I never considered us to be different from anyone else.

The first time I could put a name to what happened at home was when I was about seven years old. Mum, Kathryn and I were walking down an empty street on a Sunday. As we passed a chemist, Mum began explaining why Dad was sometimes a little angry or sad, and why he sometimes wouldn't get up in the morning. I suppose he must have been ill at the time. She told me he had something wrong in his head that meant when he was upset or stressed, things in his brain didn't add up, so he had to take a few days' rest until everything got sorted, and this problem he had was called depression and it happened to lots of people at different times.

I took all this in my stride because by that time I had obviously figured out that occasionally something happened to my daddy that I just couldn't explain. But what I couldn't accept was what my mum told me next. She said: 'Whatever happens, you have to promise me that you won't tell anybody about this depression. It has to be our secret.' Later I discovered that my mum's parents and sister knew, as did my father's parents and sister. As I became older, and the depression grew worse, Mum confided in a close friend and Dad disclosed his illness to a few colleagues at work. But at the age of seven I just couldn't grasp why I wasn't to tell anyone. I suppose I was just too naive to realise that when some people don't understand something it's easier for them to ridicule that thing and isolate it from their lives than it is to try to come to terms with what it actually involves. Because I had always lived with depression in my life I knew it was just a temporary illness, something horrible that happened to an ordinary man, who, to me, was the best father in the world.

That is why I'll always regard my childhood as a normal one, whether everyone else does or not. After all, most 'normal' children keep a diary, don't they? At least at some point. Mine started when I was about nine years old. It mainly listed things like what I had eaten for tea or that I hated my sisters because they got to stay up longer than me. In later years, my diary became an outlet for secrets, a place to write down which boy I fancied or which girl was to become my new best friend. Ordinary teenage things. But then, slowly, my diary grew into a record of this big family secret. I lived in a very smart townhouse, I went to a very good all-girls school, I had a very nice family. Everything about me was normal, ordinary, mundane even. That is, from the outside. Inside, the entire family kept Dad's secret, and I told no one except the pages of my diary.

Yet is it really so shocking? Depression is not rare, and it's not something that should be ignored, or regarded as a dangerous and contagious disease. It happens every day, to ordinary people leading ordinary lives, and it's time it was addressed and help given to those people who need it so badly. This is my family's story, which is tragic and very personal, but, sadly, not all that unique.

30 OCTOBER 2002

Today was officially the worst day of my life. Ever. I never thought it would get this bad. I always thought we'd be OK, however down he got. Today made me realise how naive I've been. I feel like I've aged about ten years and my childhood has been thrown out of the window. I mean, how can I retain any childhood innocence after I've just witnessed my dad trying to kill himself?

I think we got there just in time, unless, of course, he planned it that way. Maybe he couldn't go through with it and needed someone to stop him. I'm rambling on now; I guess it's the shock. I'll start from the beginning and explain properly. After all, you're the only one I can tell.

This morning began like any other Wednesday in October, pretty miserable and raining. Mum and I had gone to visit Emma in York to try and cheer her up after some boy problems. (I'm starting to think boyfriends might not be worth the trouble.) Dad was ill again – but not much more down than usual – so he stayed in bed this morning. We took Emma for lunch, but Mum couldn't stop worrying about Dad so we set off home early. I tried to call him a few times on the way. I think I knew when he didn't answer the phone that something was wrong.

We got home around half past three. Dad's Land Rover was on the drive. I was so annoyed with him for not making it in to work. But then Mum noticed that our car (the little green Ford Fiesta) wasn't in the drive where it should have been. We walked round the side of the house and she looked in the garage. 'Oh my God,' she said. 'The car's in the garage and your dad's inside.'

For a few seconds I didn't understand and then it suddenly hit me. I ran in front of her, jumped through the back doorway and round to the door connecting the main house to the garage. Through my tears I could see a little yellow Post-it note pushed through the key in the door. The first part in Dad's scrawl was illegible, but I could make out the bottom bit: 'Sorry. Love you all. Dad.' A suicide note.

Mum and I prised open the door to the garage but he'd barricaded it with stuff and we couldn't get in. As I screamed at him to get out of the car, I took in the scene. The hosepipe came around the side of the car and dangled in through a small gap in the driver's window. He was sitting behind the wheel. The radio was blasting to cover the roar of the engine but he could still hear our shouting. He looked up and I met his eyes. He was crying. As if in slow motion he switched off the engine and opened the door of the car. My stomach lurched and I collapsed on the floor. The relief that he was still alive washed over me but the shock that he might not have been hit me like a brick wall. What if we'd have been ten minutes later? I wanted to be sick so badly. I still feel like that now, almost disbelief that it happened. I feel as if someone *has* died.

Spent most of the afternoon crying. I didn't think I would ever stop. How could things have gone so low without me noticing? For him to think about doing that?

We got him out of the garage and sat down around the kitchen table. Even the dogs seemed to know something was wrong. Missie, our black Labrador, snuggled up to Max, our golden Labrador, and they both lay down in front of the Aga. I leaned against them both, stroking their fur because I couldn't bear to look at Dad. I couldn't believe he would let me witness that, or come home to something even worse, something unthinkable. Mum was so angry with him, mostly about the fact that I was there. But she was also incredibly upset, more so than I've ever seen her, and, my God, have I seen her cry a lot. I really couldn't see a way out of this. How could we just get up and carry on after that? But just like every other time, we talked until the cows came home, drank sweet tea for our shock, and the cracks began to heal themselves. Always the same solution but I know it won't last for long. The nasty fuck keeps coming back to mess him up. Will he go all the way next time?

He's not been this low in a long time – well, actually, maybe it's not that long ago. It was at the end of July, I think, or the beginning of August when he was last really down. That was the day he just disappeared. Again, it had started out like an ordinary working day (for Dad, at least; the rest of us were on summer holiday from school). He had gone into work, suit on, briefcase in hand. It was about mid-morning before we realised anything was wrong. Andy (one of his colleagues) had rung to see if Dad was coming in today. We were worried obviously, because we presumed that if he hadn't arrived in the office then he must have been involved in an accident on the way. We tried his mobile phone, but it was switched off. We rang the police, the hospitals, everyone we could think of. The hospitals had no record of him or anyone matching his description being brought in, and the police had not been alerted to any accidents involving his car. We were also told by the police that we had to wait twenty-four hours until we could report him missing. Hours later we still couldn't get in touch with him, and there were no signs as to his whereabouts. Kathryn and her boyfriend Nick were in the Lake District on holiday at the time and came home early when we phoned with our concerns. By the time the two of them arrived home there was a police patrol vehicle outside. Mum had become more and more hysterical and had phoned the police again, this time informing them that she had reason to believe he might harm himself. So there we were, my sisters and me, Mum, Nick and two police officers all standing around the kitchen table. In the awkward silence that filled the gaps in the chaotic conversation, I faintly heard an engine, which grew louder and louder until it was recognisable as Dad's diesel Land Rover. It roared past the window of the kitchen and pulled on to the drive. Dad rushed in, concerned about the police car in front of the house. It was only when he saw us all standing there that he realised the police were there because of him. He simply started crying.

It turned out that he had set off to work and then decided on the way that he couldn't face it. Instead of turning round and coming home he had gone for a drive to try and sort his head out. After driving for some time he had got so mentally and physically exhausted that he had pulled over in a lay-by and gone to sleep, and that was where he had stayed all day until he woke in a panic and rushed home because he knew he was late. He had no idea of the chaos and commotion he caused because he was so blind to anyone else's feelings but his own.

But that day was nothing compared to the situation we found ourselves in today.

The strangest thing about it all was this evening. Mum and I took Dad into the office in the hope that sorting out his room would make him more optimistic about going back to work. While he was buried in paperwork, we went over the road to the newsagent to buy lottery tickets. I come to this newsagent all the time to buy sweets for Dad and me when I'm cleaning his office after school. Standing in that queue was just so unbelievably surreal. It's like going to work when you've just murdered someone. We were so calm and acted if everything was completely normal, and even by our twisted standards it most definitely wasn't a normal situation. But lottery tickets? I mean, why the hell did we think it was our lucky day? Safe to say, we didn't win.

God. I'm so screwed up I don't even know what to say. I can't ever look at him the same way again. Why would he want me to see that? I'm fourteen years old. Is it selfish of me to want a parent who worries about me and what I'm doing rather than the other way round? More than anything I can't understand why he would ever want to die, to leave us behind. Are we not enough for him? Does he not love me the way I love him? He can't. My love for him feels pointless now because I know however much I do and however much I show him my feelings, it's not enough to combat his depression.

My friends rang to see if I wanted to go round and watch a film. It's half-term and that is, after all, what normal fourteen-year-olds do in the holidays. How can I explain to them I've got much bigger things to worry about right now? Mum doesn't want me to tell anyone, not even my sisters. My own flesh and blood, and I can't even tell them their stupid prat of a dad wanted to kill himself today. It's not too difficult because Emma's away at uni till Christmas and Kathryn's still down in Cambridge for a while, but I tell Rach everything and she'll be back home tomorrow. I have to lie and pretend everything's OK when inside I'm falling apart. Life's really not fair.

Gonna go to bed. I can't stop crying and it's not doing me any good. Supposed to be spending the day doing homework tomorrow but it all seems so insignificant now. I hate him so much, but I love him, too, and want nothing more than for us all to be together and happy, just the six of us. Will it ever be possible?

2 NOVEMBER 2002

Everything just seems to have rolled back to its usual place. It's as if the dark cloud has lifted from above our house. A few days ago Dad was trying to poison himself with carbon monoxide; now it's hard to believe he's the same man. He's been into the office and he comes home and tells jokes at teatime. He's paying special attention to me as well because I think he feels guilty for what happened the other day. I don't care. I'm just so pleased he's back again. His eyes have lost their glazed look and I can have a real hug rather than cuddling a stiff, sobbing body.

Rachel's back home but I'm still not allowed to tell her what happened. Mum says she's too stressed out with her A-levels, and because she's having such a rough time at school with friends and a boy who messed her around Mum thinks she won't be able to cope. What she doesn't realise is that maybe I can't cope. I need to talk to her, tell her exactly how it felt to be standing there, praying to God that he would get out of the car.

Mum just wants me to put it to the back of my mind, to stop thinking about it, because, after all, he's better now. That's just what it's like in this house; everything revolves around Dad and his illness. If he's down, then the rest of us feel like we're walking on eggshells. Mum must have seen him down hundreds of times, but she never stops trying with him. I get annoyed after a few minutes of the conversation going round in circles, yet she's so patient with him and can talk for hours in the hope that she'll eventually get through. At one point I asked myself how she could stay with him, when it made her so miserable. I know part of the reason is us four, but looking at her when he's down I know it's because she believes the love they have for each other will always beat any dark day he has, and most of the time, it does. The only way I can put the other day out of my head is to believe that he didn't intend to go through with it. That maybe it was a cry for attention. That things were worse than we had realised and somehow he needed to show us that. If I let myself think that he actually didn't want to be here any more then I couldn't carry on.

I'm just so glad he's back to his usual self, even if it is just a twisted form of joy, stemming from the realisation that he's still alive. Maybe it's like a near-death experience; even though it was self-inflicted he must feel some kind of euphoria at being alive. I miss this person that's here now, this funny, caring, active Dad, and I hate the way he gets taken away and replaced by a lifeless body. I just wish there could be some kind of cure. If he could be this way all the time, our family would be normal; better than that even, we'd be perfect. I mean, of course we'd still have flaws, but every family does. Depression is more than a flaw; it's a weed that, even when you try to suppress it, keeps growing back, and it sometimes gets out of control. I just hope we can suppress it for a while this time because I don't want Dad to go away again.

Back at school on Monday. Haven't done any schoolwork and I'll probably get into trouble. I can't even explain to the teachers that I've had other stuff going on. This is our secret and nobody can ever know. I've kept it a secret for so long I don't actually know how people will react. I've heard people talk about 'crazies', 'nutjobs' and 'headcases', but would they really see my dad like that? The man that dresses in a smart suit, goes into work every day with a smile on his face and a cheesy joke to tell? Who knows? But he wants it to be kept a secret so that's how it stays. I'll just have to do what I always do – smile and make up some excuse. I can't have our perfect Brady Bunch exterior tarnished, now can I?

4 NOVEMBER 2002

So excited. Today has been a good day! Went into Mum's school for the day – a private all-girls school near Hessle – as she needed to do some display boards during half-term. On the staff room door there was a notice about a trip the school was running to Madagascar with a company called World Challenge Expeditions. It's a month-long trip that leaves on 1 July 2004. I'm not sure why but I was attracted to it straight away. I've only just found out where Madagascar is (an island off the south coast of Africa) and it seems so far, so exotic. Just the thought of getting away from here and doing something new really appeals to me. The trip is being run by the head of Geography so Mum sent him an email tonight and he said it's fine for me to come because they've still got places. How exciting! It's very scary, though. I'd be going with girls who I've never met before. Plus, I have to raise £3,125 to be able to go. That's a hell of a lot of money.

But how good would it be? Something that I could do myself, completely on my own. No one would be able to compare this to anything Kathryn, Emma and Rachel have done. This is something new that I could do for me. I can't wait. I really hope it works out. Got the first meeting just before Christmas when I'll get to meet the other girls who are going.

12 NOVEMBER 2002

Oh, how stupid am I? I always let my hopes build up that he's going to be OK, but already he's back down again. You start to notice it happening just before it actually hits; it's the same every time. His eyes glaze over completely and start to sag somewhat. He falls asleep anywhere and everywhere, becomes withdrawn and quiet, and begins to lose his appetite. You can tell as soon as you look at him whether or not he is well. As soon as she knows he is ill, Mum gets into her routine.

Out come the bananas, the vitamins, the glasses of orange juice, the stuffed vegetable meals and, most importantly, the chocolate (releases those happy little fellas called endorphins). But by that time it's probably too late anyway. He has gone, slipped away into oblivion, and there is nothing we can do except wait until he comes back.

It's always the same reason as well. He keeps telling us the business isn't working and that he'll either have to sell up or declare himself bankrupt. I can't help thinking he's being overdramatic. It sounds stupid, I know – I mean, an accountant should really know if his own business is working – but I refuse to let him just give up. There are so many options, but he almost seems to want to fail. He can't just give up, though, because there's not just him to think about. Mum went to the doctor's with him today; he's been put on a new drug, which, hopefully, will have some dramatic results. I hope it does because I can see the strain on Mum already. I want to be able to support her fully but I'm still only young myself, and I don't think she can tell me everything she's thinking. On second thoughts, perhaps I wouldn't want to know. If she said she was going to leave Dad I don't think I could handle that. Dad really would just give up if she wasn't there.

In other areas life's not too great, either. Grandad's been diagnosed with a benign tumour on his spine. He's deteriorating quite a lot and it's hard on Mum, as Grandad's always been the one she talks to, especially since Grandma died. He's there for us four, too. I miss our Wednesday teatime visits to his flat in Beverley; he was ace at cooking, and always managed to cheer us up with his lasagne and cherry crumble. He can't really cook any more, though, and there's hardly enough room to swing a cat in his new flat in Elloughton. It's awful to watch him, like he's slowly slipping away, when he was always so full of life, so cheerful. It's almost as if he's waiting to be taken. He cries sometimes and says he just wants to die so he can be in heaven and see Grandma again. I hope he does see her, even though I don't think I even believe in heaven.

Hopefully he'll be OK to come to Florida with us; that might cheer him up a bit. I'm really looking forward to that. I have some vague notion that a holiday might do us all some good, even though it'll put extra pressure on the money situation, too.

On Sunday Kathryn broke her ankle in a uni rugby match and so has come home for the week; she's spending her time lying on the sofa watching the Rugby Tri-Nations on TV while Dad drifts in and out of consciousness beside her. At least I can escape at school, even though I spend most of the day dreading coming home (and I have mock exams next week).

When Dad's not at work or can't pick us up, Rach and I get the train from Beverley to Brough, our nearest station, after school. We spend most of the train journey betting on what the situation will be like when we get home. It sounds horrible but to us it's pretty normal and just a waiting game until he comes out the other side. The train journey is actually a bright and busy time, spent talking and laughing. Then we step out onto the platform at Brough and it's as if a dark cloud has come down to engulf us. It stays with us all the way home where it takes its usual place over the roof of the house.

I'm gonna really miss Rach when she goes to uni. It will be just me, Mum and Dad at home, a scary thought. Anyway I've got to go; tea's ready and I have to rescue Kathryn from boredom downstairs. Will write soon. Hopefully things will soon be looking up.

Still no luck with boys. Everyone at school seems to be going out with someone; some girls even reckon they're sleeping with their boyfriends (at fourteen, just wrong). Not that I'd want to do that. I mean, I'd be happy if someone just looked at me. Feel pretty ugly and I reckon I've stopped growing, too. Surely I can't be 5ft 2in for the rest of my life? It's such an embarrassing height.

19 NOVEMBER 2002

Sadly, still no good news. It seems to be dragging on this time and today was one of the worst days. He was so angry. It started out with him and Mum having a huge row about money (what's new?) and about Florida. He said he wasn't coming because we'd all be better off without him, plus it would save money him being at home and able to work. What a stupid, annoying idiot he is sometimes. How on earth could we go away for Christmas without him?

Anyway, the argument carried on during the journey to school when Rach asked him why he wasn't coming. He really went off on one, ranting and raving about how we knew nothing and didn't care about money, and that all we wanted was a holiday et cetera. That's not the case at all and he knows it. God, I mean, I'm fourteen and I spend half my time worrying about my dad's business and our family debt. He was so, so horrible, though. I just burst into tears. I can handle the blues, the desperate stage, but when he gets angry and bitter and starts taking it out on us it really frustrates me.

He's always been fairly strict with us but never really angry or violent. The only other time I can remember him being that mad was when he was coming out of an 'episode'. I was really young, maybe seven, and we'd just got a new computer table which had been marked by a big cup of hot Ribena. The dark purple stain left on the brand-new wood sent Dad crazy and he shouted at us all. No one would own up to doing it and eventually he narrowed it down to either me or Rachel. Still neither of us admitted anything, so Dad went upstairs and fetched a blue leather belt. He started with me; a few sharp hits round the back of the legs. I screamed in pain and could hear Emma and Kathryn crouched halfway up the stairs, sobbing. Rachel shouted out that she was to blame and to stop hitting me. To this day I don't know if she actually had done it or if she just wanted to stop me being hurt. Either way, she got punished and had the red marks to prove it. Somehow it was justified, though, because of the way he was feeling. We all said it was OK and put it to the back of our minds because under 'normal circumstances' he wouldn't have responded like that.

Today he was just as mad, although we're too old for sharp slaps round the legs now. Maybe that would have been better than the rejection Rachel and I felt. He seemed so disgusted with us he wouldn't even take us all the way to school; we were dropped off in the middle of town and had to make our way to the bus station. Rachel sat and hugged me on a mouldy wet bench while I sobbed on her shoulder. I was scared, not of him physically, but what would happen if he meant what he said, that he wouldn't come on holiday and that he actually did think those things about us. I've always tried to be understanding and not ask too much of Mum and Dad, but maybe I haven't tried hard enough.

We were both really late for school and I tried to go into the toilets to sort myself out before French but it was pointless; everyone could see from my puffy eyes and sniffly nose that I'd been crying. Miss Cairns didn't say anything but I could tell she was wondering what was wrong.

After the lesson I ran and found my friend Abby and just burst into tears again. I wanted to tell her everything but found myself choking up out of loyalty to Dad. I just told her there'd been an argument and that I was upset. She consoled me but obviously it wasn't enough.

I spent all day wondering how Dad was and hoping he hadn't done anything stupid. I love him even though he hurts us sometimes. I know deep down it's not him talking and that he's only angry and frustrated with himself and what he cannot control. I just wish he didn't take it out on us.

When I got home tonight he apologised for the way he acted, but Rach is still mad at him. She holds a grudge sometimes! He still says he's not coming to Florida. Maybe when he gets better he'll change his mind. If he gets better. This time it looks as though it's never going to end.

I'll find out my mock results next week. Really hope I've done OK. Can't believe it's GCSEs next year. I really feel I'm going downhill at school. It all seems so pointless. Kathryn's gone back to Cambridge. She breaks up first week in December, though, so will be coming home then, Florida or not.

1 DECEMBER 2002

It's Sunday night. I've just come back from a really lovely weekend in Cambridge visiting Kathryn. It was the St John's Christmas service on the Friday night (which is recorded for BBC radio), so Mum, Dad and I travelled down on Friday afternoon. The journey was completed in the embarrassment that is the giant noisy Land Rover, with Dad consuming an entire packet of mint imperials and he and Mum singing along to some ridiculous tape. I was due to stay with Kathryn in her room in college; Mum and Dad had their own room in the city centre.

When we arrived in Cambridge we weren't entirely sure how to get to Kathryn's college because the centre is completely closed off to traffic except taxis and buses. Mum, who was driving at this point, decided to head towards the town centre anyway so we could park in the college. There were CCTV cameras watching the roads, though, and as soon as the car approached the pedestrian area, bollards began to rise up out of the road, blocking our path. Mum panicked and screamed at Dad to do something. We all turned round and saw a long line of taxis and buses behind us. The car was completely blocked in.

Dad had been half snoozing in the passenger seat and woke up to the sound of Mum shrieking. He found the whole situation hilarious and just sat there giggling. Mum got out of her seat and walked around to Dad's side of the car, banging on the window and begging him to come and sort out the problem. She couldn't stifle her laughter between her embarrassed shouts. During this time I was on the phone to Kathryn explaining what had happened and trying to get out of view of the pedestrians who had gathered round the car and were staring at us. Dad eventually got into the driver's seat and managed to turn the car around to get us out of our trap. It was so embarrassing, but hilarious at the same time. The taxis were beeping and shouting at Mum, who had turned a shade of deep red. Dad just found the whole thing too funny and made sure Mum wasn't allowed to forget it for the whole weekend.

The service itself was held in St John's own chapel. It's such an old beautiful building but it was absolutely freezing in there and I could not stop shivering. We got really good seats, though, because Kathryn still has a cast on her ankle and is on crutches. We were very close to the choir and I was still in a giggly mood from the car journey before so couldn't help laughing at the men's high-pitched voices. Immature, I know, but I'm sure anyone else would have done the same. Kathryn kept glaring at me, though – she makes me feel so guilty sometimes – and I was silent pretty soon after that.

We went out after the service to a little Italian restaurant called La Galleria and although it was expensive Dad didn't seem to mind and was on really good form all night. It was so nice just to chat about ordinary things and not be worried about him being down or thinking that we couldn't really afford to be there, especially after all the recent arguments about the trip to Florida and the business. We just had a really lovely meal, with nice food and drink and excellent company.

That night, back at the college, I spent ages talking to Kathryn and watching TV. It was just so nice to spend some quality time with her. Since she's gone to uni I've felt that the age gap between us, even though it's only five years, has become a really big deal. I felt for a long time that maybe she'd outgrown me and that she wasn't bothered about spending time with me any more. I was proven wrong on Friday, though, and I realised how much I miss her. It's making me think about Rachel leaving home next year now; I hope we don't grow apart in the same way.

Saturday was spent shopping in Cambridge, and Mum bought me a really cool jumper from a place called CULT. It sells alternative clothing, really original stuff that you wouldn't find anywhere else, but Kathryn wasn't too convinced; she thinks it's a shop for skater kids or people who are into weird music. She's just not very cool. Brought most of her stuff back with us today so that she doesn't have to struggle with it on the train. She's meeting Dad at Twickenham next week to go and see the Varsity rugby match. Sounds boring, if you ask me, but maybe it will be good for Dad. He's been on top form for the last couple of weeks, so anything that keeps him like that is worth it.

11 DECEMBER 2002

Just come home from my first meeting for the trip to Madagascar. It was so nerve-racking. I left school a bit early, and Dad gave me a lift to Mum's school because the meeting was due to start at half past four. I was really nervous. Most people were already in the room. I really didn't want to go in and – I feel like such an idiot thinking about it now – started crying. I was just so scared about meeting them all.

Mum eventually persuaded me to go in but when I did it was so obvious that I'd been upset and I felt ridiculous. Mum stayed with me for the first few minutes while everyone introduced themselves to me, but then she had to leave so we could get the meeting started. I'm such a retard. I mean, I'm fourteen, I should be able to do these things by myself now and not be so scared of daft things like meeting new people. As it turned out, and as you would expect, they were all really nice to me, overly nice, in fact, probably because I'd been crying and looked like a little kid.

There are about twenty of us in all, including four other girls my age, three in the year above and about ten or eleven in year twelve. They are very nice people but are all very confident and seem to know each other so well. I guess that's what comes from going to a very small, all-girls private school. Or maybe that's just my prejudices talking. I think everyone has an idea of what a person is going to be like before you meet them. Perhaps they have their own views about what a girl from a state school is like. Maybe I should just get to know them and see what happens.

Anyway, the meeting was taken by a man from World Challenge Expeditions. He basically talked us through what we could do on the trip and how it was us who actually created the route and decided on an itinerary. We have to do some kind of community work during the month; this can be teaching, building, conservation work or just a visit to a community centre in the area. He showed us some photos from another trip where a group went to Africa and helped to build a village school. It looked amazing. Then we can choose where to trek, if we go north or south, and whether to visit cities or villages, rainforest or mountains. It was all so exciting.

We also discussed fundraising. I half expected most of them to say that the money wasn't going to be a problem, but it turned out most of them were just as worried as I was, if not more so. They came up with ideas for raffles, quizzes, bag-packing events, formal dinners. By the end we had hundreds of fundraising ideas on the list. I think I'll ask at school if I can set up a stall at lunchtime selling sweets or cakes or something. I can't believe I'm actually doing this. Halfway around the world all on my own for a whole month. To tell you the truth, I'm terrified. Half of me thinks I'm being ridiculous and wants to back out, but the other half is jumping up and down in excitement already!

17 DECEMBER 2002

Happy birthday to me, happy birthday to me, happy birthday, dear Sarah, happy birthday to me! Fifteen years old. God, that feels ancient. Didn't get many presents, just some art materials and a few books, but everyone came and sang round my bed, and that's the best bit about birthdays. I know money's tight too and with us going away I don't mind not getting much. Yes, you heard right, *we are* going away after all! Let's just say Mum doesn't let things lie, and she kept on at Dad that he had to come otherwise he would ruin the holiday for the rest of us. Plus, we have Grandad with us this time and I think that was the selling point; he would feel too guilty leaving her to deal with that on her own. Kathryn's also in a wheelchair this time, which is ace because it means we won't have to queue for the rides at Disney. Dad's actually been a lot better recently, just stressed out because of stupid tax returns. God, if I ever meet this taxman that people talk about then he'll have a lot to answer for!

This weekend was really good. Had some friends over and Dad dropped us off in York to do some shopping, I bought a blue Golddigga bag and some jeans. We went for lunch at Bella Pasta as well and we all felt really old! Then Dad picked us all up again and we came home and had a sleepover. We watched *Roadkill*, which I thought was really scary but obviously didn't say so (everyone else would have thought I was a right wimp!). All in all, it was a really good day. We had the sleepover up in the attic room and stayed awake until really early Sunday morning, eating sweets and chocolate. Felt like I was one of the group and it was so lovely them all coming to see my house cos they all thought it was huge and really impressive.

The house is still quite new to us, though. We moved in the summer of 2001 to this village, Elloughton, because Dad wanted somewhere that would take him away from his work and give us all better health. But I'd gladly give it up if I could guarantee we'd all be happy. Having the nice things, the holidays and a nice house, are like islands of calm weather in a storm. They just make things better for a short while. Even so, I can't wait to go on holiday now. Really feel like things are improving for me. Maybe next year will be the year I finally get a boyfriend and be all skinny and popular. Then again, maybe not. I think I'd just settle for the boyfriend part!

3 JANUARY 2003

Just got back from Florida this morning. It was amazing. Last time we went at Christmas I was too young to remember most of it, but this time I was old enough to go on all the big rides and it was sooo good. The best one is the 'Rock 'n' Roller Coaster' sponsored by the band Aerosmith, and it does 0–60 mph in 2.8 seconds. Mum hated it and had her eyes shut the whole time, but that just added to the entertainment for us four. I say 'us four' because that was the day Dad stayed at the villa with Grandad, who was pretty exhausted and needed a day off. Dad, on the other hand, had been getting more and more worked up about these bloody tax returns, so much so that Mum told him to stay behind. So it was just the five of us at MGM studios and although it was good it just didn't feel quite right.

They have this area of MGM where they do the filming for the New York shots of the Disney films; it's a black and white backdrop with shops and cafés along a main street. At Christmas they give you all these 3D glasses so it looks like the fake snow they produce is really falling from the sky. There was a Mickey's Coffee Shop on the corner and we all got coffee or hot chocolate to add to the cold weather effect, but walking down that street, even with all the lights, the snow and the warming sensation from the hot drinks, I couldn't help feel like something was missing, and it was. It didn't feel complete without Dad. Whenever there were five of us it felt as though there should be six. We just weren't 'Team Griffin' without him. It made me realise that's what it's like every time he's ill, because even though he is physically there throughout those times, it's as if he's missing in spirit, and without him fully there, we're just not whole.

New Year's Eve was classic Griffin family magic, though. It all went wrong in the most comical way. The day started out pretty well. We decided to spend it in Epcot so we could bring in the New Year in one of the country-themed restaurants situated around the lake they call 'the Earth'. We had phoned up that morning to reserve a table, but the only reservation we could get was in the German restaurant where they were holding their annual beer festival. Not ideal, but better than nothing. The night grew closer and it looked like rain, but Dad promised us it was going to be 'just a shower that would soon pass'. We found a spot on the side of the lake to watch the New Year firework display before our meal; luckily, it was close to a hot dog vendor's parasol. The rain started off lightly but slowly got heavier, and the five of us and our two wheelchairs edged closer to the umbrella. Dad insisted again that it was just a shower and that it would pass. An hour later we were still hunched under the umbrella, water pouring over its edges into the laps of our wheelchair-bound relatives. Emma was wearing a brand-new denim skirt and the dark dye in the fabric began to run; her legs were soon tinted an attractive shade of Smurf blue.

We then decided to make a dash for 'Germany' to see if our table was ready, so we ran and wheeled our way there, and took shelter in the 'traditional German toyshop', which sold only handmade wooden toys and the customary Disney 'mac-in-a-sac', available in either powder blue or sunshine yellow. It turned out the table wasn't ready because the revellers inside, obviously enjoying the beer festival a little too much, didn't want to come out into 'just a shower', which had actually turned into a major thunderstorm. Two hours later we were still sheltering in the German toyshop, getting increasingly annoyed with the Disney cuckoo clocks and the mooing wooden cows. Eventually, at ten to midnight on New Year's Eve, we gave up all hope and abandoned the wooden toys, leaving Germany with a feeling of great disappointment. Rushing toward Epcot's exit, we heard the sound of fireworks exploding and clocks chiming, and stopped under the nearest shelter to wish each other a Happy New Year. It took me a few minutes to realise where we were. We had brought in the New Year outside a block of toilets, albeit Epcot's space-themed toilets, complete with Mickey and Minnie in spacesuits. Not quite the start to 2003 that we had hoped for, but funny and fitting to our family none-the-less.

Luckily everyone saw the funny side, and we stopped at the twenty-four-hour supermarket on the way back to the villa to buy tortilla chips and alcohol, the way to celebrate the New Year in style!

The next night we went to the Peabody hotel in Orlando for a meal and pretended it was New Year's Eve all over again. It was a really lovely place, decorated in monochrome, and really posh. I just hope our rather pathetic false start to 2003 isn't a reflection of the year ahead. I have high hopes for this year, with my GCSEs and the beginning of life at home with Mum and Dad while the other three are at uni. I'm apprehensive but positive, too. Maybe Dad will improve this year. It's also Mum and Dad's twenty-fifth wedding anniversary in July. You can't get that far without actually loving each other, now can you?

3 FEBRUARY 2003

For once (thank God) I can report that things at home are actually OK. It's so noticeable that the mood of the house revolves around whether or not Dad is well, so it's pretty obvious that of late he's been fairly high-spirited. He completed all his tax returns on time and is finally feeling positive about the business. Mum and Dad have even been talking about replacing the Vauxhall Zafira with a new car, maybe even a new Land Rover, which is a major thing, especially considering the heavy discussions about money we had before going to Florida. I really hope the money situation is improving. I know Rachel's worried about going to Sheffield uni in September because of the financial strain it will put on us. She can't put her life on hold, though.

Emma reckons one of the reasons Dad is so positive right now is because of an emotional chat they had on Saturday night. Emma's had, well, how can I say this, 'worries' since she was about sixteen. She found her A-levels really hard work, and the pressure of exams, coupled with these social worries, was the final straw. God, that sounds awful, I sound really ignorant. Next I'll be saying she went a bit loopy and calling her a nutcase. But that's not what it's like at all. She was just finding stuff really difficult at the time, and balancing everything all at once was becoming a major issue. Soon after she turned seventeen she started seeing a mental health nurse at home. She was called Rita. Breathing exercises and diet regimes became the order of the day, followed by our GP introducing her to anti-depressants to get her over the bad times.

Just before this she cut herself for the first time, in the middle of one of our famous soap-opera 'scenes'. It was the night before Kathryn was due to go to Cambridge. We were in the lounge and discussing 'things' (money, jobs, the point of life). Dad was on the sofa, ignoring our pleadings for him to talk. Emma then came down the stairs with a huge cut across her lower arm, the tears streaming down her face and mixing with the dark blood pouring from the wound. She showed it to Dad, shouting, 'Look! Look! This is what it takes to get your attention. This is what you make me do.' In response Dad just cried and buried himself deeper into the sofa, but with hindsight I can see how, in his then state of mind, it might not have helped.

But I often wonder if Emma is maybe justified in blaming Dad a little bit for her health worries. I mean, I'm no scientist, I'm only fifteen, but when Emma sees Dad dealing with his problems in such a way, does she subconsciously copy him? Or are depression and other such illnesses hereditary? If that's the case, could I start experiencing similar issues? Shit. I hope not. All I know is that she, like every one else, has her problems. I just worry more about her because of Dad.

Some people reckon offspring act in a certain way in reaction to their parents' behaviour, often doing everything in their power to be the opposite of their mum and dad. It just so happens that Emma's behaviour is similar to Dad's (even if hers is on a much lower scale). So, is it better to hide adult problems from your children, to avoid fucking up their lives as well? Or is it better to share your problems with them in the hope that they will learn from them and so that you can support each other through the bad times? Perhaps it doesn't matter either way, because if your children are genetically predestined to follow in your footsteps then there might be nothing you can do to prevent it.

Who knows? I guess I just have to live my life and hope for the best. I only hope I'm not screwed up already. Philip Larkin definitely knew what he was talking about. Kind of a depressing thought, though. Maybe I won't have kids. I'm too scared they'll turn out like me!

Anyway, back to Emma. She turns nineteen next week and it's her first birthday in York, so Kathryn and Rachel have said they'll go over to see her. I'm too young still (*and still* 5ft 2in) so there's no way I'd get into the clubs and stuff. They're having a fancy dress weekend, I think; males dress as females and vice versa. Kathryn's going as a surgeon and Rachel's borrowing Wayne's outfit and going as a paratrooper. Wayne's Rachel's ex, by the way. Not sure if I've mentioned him in this diary before. He's a family friend and is such a nice guy, but he's been madly in love with Rachel for ages and to be honest it's a bit weird because he's been friends with all my sisters for a long time (he went out with Emma for a bit, I think!). He likes her a ridiculous amount. But he does buy her loads of soft toys, chocolates and jewellery. (Guess that's the nice part about having a boyfriend – not that I'd know!) Some of the lads are going as nuns – a bit strange but sounds fun. Anyway, wish I was going to be there.

Valentine's Day soon and all my sisters have boyfriends. It's really annoying cos I know I won't even get a card or anything. Mum keeps telling me I'm only young and I've still got time, but I still feel a bit of a geek at school when everyone else is 'seeing' or even going out with a boy. Never mind, maybe I'll get a surprise card from someone. Kathryn sent me one when I was little. She posted it through the front door and pretended it was from a boy at my infant school. They all teased me about it so much that I got really angry and burst into tears. Kathryn then confessed it was from her and that angered me even more because she'd obviously felt sorry for me in the first place. God, how embarrassing. I'll keep my fingers crossed anyway and let you know if some hot boy sends me a card declaring his undying love. Unlikely, I know, but a girl can dream, can't she?

Less than eighteen months until Madagascar! Been selling sweets at school and have so far managed to raise about £400. Not bad but still got a *very* long way to go.

4 MARCH 2003

Just read my last diary entry and no, I didn't get any cards, surprise surprise. Got bigger things to worry about right now anyway, and for the first in a long time it's not about Dad.

Been feeling really left out at home lately. I can see the gap between me and the others getting wider and wider, and even though they all seem to be getting older I feel as though I'm staying the same age and that we have nothing in common any more. I've never really been bothered about having very close friends at school because I've always been able to come home and have my three best friends right there. But since Emma's birthday (when they all went out together and yours truly stayed home alone) Rachel's been more and more distant, and even though I've tried talking to her about it there's not a lot she can do. I mean, she's going off to do her own thing next year and I'll be staying at home with nothing but three more years of school to look forward to. Rachel and Emma have just booked a holiday to Ibiza for the summer as well because Rachel felt like she missed out when Emma and Kathryn went to Faliraki last summer. 'What about me?' I feel like screaming. 'Who wants to go on holiday with me?' No one, it seems – well, apart from Mum and Dad, but they have to take me even if they don't want to! All three of them are going to the St John's Ball in June as well. They're all getting their hair and make-up done before the event and are staying over at Kathryn's afterwards. I just feel so young all the time and that they're not interested in me any more. They try to be kind because I think Rachel's told them all how I'm feeling, but I don't want their sympathy. I just want my big sisters back. Growing up sucks. People get older and then they just abandon you to grow up all by yourself.

Can't really talk to Mum about it at the minute, either. Think she's feeling pretty quiet and is keeping herself to herself. It would have been Auntie Susan's birthday tomorrow and it's ten years since she died. I can't really go and talk to her about sisters when the age gap between her and Susan was eight years, more than between any of us, and she has a real reason to miss her sister. I don't know what I'd do if I lost any of the other three, not to mention if anything happened to Mum or Dad. It's too painful to think about. Yet Mum's lost her younger sister and her mum, and she still seems so strong. I don't understand how she keeps going. She really amazes me sometimes. She's doing really well at work, too. She's just been told that the school will be merging with another one next year, but she's taken it all really well and is even going for the deputy head position. I hope I'm half the person she is when I'm older, especially when I think of everything she has to handle with Dad.

It's weird how one person seems to have to cope with so much when other people appear to coast through life without any problems. But you never know all of what is going on behind closed doors. Many people look to be coasting through life, but although they appear fine on the surface, they might be bubbling with fear, worry and pain underneath. I suppose it teaches you not to judge people on the outside. On the other hand, I can't help thinking that some people are just ridiculously lucky. The other girls who are going to Madagascar, for example, all look as though they don't have a care in the world. Then again, I probably look like that on the outside, and Mum doesn't go around shouting her problems from the rooftops, either.

Oh, by the way, we did get a new car, a Land Rover Freelander. Dad surprised Mum at the dealership and got her a personalised number plate for it. It's C6 GCA. The C6G for Carol Griffin and GCA for Dad's company so Dad can use it for the business, too. It was really cool because she had no idea and was really shocked when she saw it. I love it when he does stuff like that. It reminds me how much he loves her.

29 MAY 2003

Just got back home from school. It's pretty late cos I had to wait for Dad to finish with some clients before I could get a lift back. Rachel is on study leave at the minute and so it's just me at school. I'm still cleaning the office as a job, so it makes sense for me to do it during the week after school rather than have to come in again at a weekend. I don't mind being at the office anyway, it's quite nice. When I arrive, Dad sometimes has a client in his office; if so I'll sit in the meeting room and read *The Times* (or try the quick crossword) and make coffee for everyone. If he's in and not busy I'll go in and chat with him, and usually get some money for a quick trip to the newsagent. It's sweets for me and a Lion or a Mars bar for Dad. Sometimes he asks for a Marathon bar – apparently that's what Snickers used to be called. I swear he's stuck in the past sometimes. The other day I was labelling envelopes in reception and noticed that after all the single men's names he had written 'esquire'. I didn't even know people still did that. It's ancient writing!

Even if Dad's not in the office, there's always some money in the drawer so I can go into town. After I've read the paper I might do some homework or play on Dad's computer before eventually starting to clean. I hate that job with a passion! It takes so long to do and its never clean enough for Dad, he's such a perfectionist. I need the money, though, so can't complain. After all, I'm getting a tenner each week for something that only takes me a couple of hours. Dad was in a really good mood today, so it wasn't too bad, and on the way home he went the long way around Walkington with all the windows on the Land Rover down and the *Evita* musical tape on ridiculously loud. And then he started singing along! God, I didn't know whether to laugh or die from embarrassment. He really cannot sing.

It's half past eight now and I've still got lots of homework to do. I have to show my technology coursework by the end of the month. I'm sitting on the big window sill in my room, staring out at the road. You can tell it's summer because it's slowly been getting lighter and lighter every night. I love just chilling out here, watching the world go by and hearing the rush of traffic on the A63. To be honest, there's not much of the world going by at the end of a cul-de-sac in a tiny village but still, it's nice to people-watch. Plus, this window sill is perfect for dancing on. I was in such a good mood after the journey home I stuck on my *All Time Greatest Movies* CD and sang along to Barry White's 'My First, My

Last, My Everything'. It's one of those tunes you can just scream along to and dance really badly and no one will care (probably a good thing about living at the end of a cul-de-sac). Maybe I'm weird because I like my own company. Is it that odd to enjoy sitting around by yourself and dancing on window sills to cheesy music? At least if you only depend on yourself for company you're never going to be disappointed! Maybe writing this diary in itself is weird. I mean, perhaps I should be telling someone else all these random thoughts. Then again, maybe not. The thought of someone else being given a window to see inside my head is pretty scary!

Rachel's been in revising a lot the last few weeks so have got to see her and just hang around doing girly things. I think she's realised that when she moves out in September, I won't just be there all the time like I am now. That's the good thing about sisters. They're like friends who share a lot of the same things that you do and you can never get rid of them. You're happy and they share that with you; you get upset and they instantly know why, or at least let you snot all over their shoulder while you tell them. God, should stop getting all soppy now; another thing about sisters is that they steal everything from your room and they may well get their hands on this diary!

2 JUNE 2003

Feeling really down. Things at school are getting horrible and I still feel left out at home, despite Rachel being around more, so I just feel really isolated. I'm not sure what's happened at school; it kind of all seemed to fall apart at once.

I have always been really close friends with Abby, but more recently she's been spending a lot of time at the park by her house, with some guys that live near her and a girl called Michelle. Michelle and I have been friends for ages because her sister is in the same year as Emma. But because I don't live in Beverley any more they're just meeting all the time without me and, get this, they've both started smoking! They go down to the park on a night and just sit around and drink and smoke. I'm not saying I'd want to be there doing that with them, but it would be nice to be invited, and I just feel like they're growing up and doing new things without me. They're meeting new people, too. Jess, another friend, has been going out with this one guy for a while, and his friends (who are all a year older) all hang out around the park, too, talking and getting to know all my friends. I just feel there is this whole other world that I'm now not a part of, and at school it's really obvious that the distance is growing between us.

I just don't know what to do. I don't want to get involved with the whole park thing because I think if Mum and Dad found out they'd be really disappointed in me. Plus, I don't really see the point in it. I've always been able to drink at parties at home so that's never been much of an issue. I don't see the attraction of drinking in secret. I just hate feeling as left out and lonely as I do right now. At school everyone just talks about what they did last night or who snogged which guy. I feel completely out of the loop and so angry with Abby. I really miss her; we were such close friends.

15 JUNE 2003

I'm really terrified. A few days ago I was having a bath when I noticed a tiny lump in my right boob. I know when you're a girl you're supposed to do breast exams and stuff so that you notice any changes, but this was something I just spotted when getting washed, and it was really weird, all gristly and hard. I felt OK about it at first, thought it was some kind of growth thing or maybe was just supposed to be there. I mean, I've never felt anyone else's chest so how do I know mine is any different? But then I told Mum about it and she got really worried and said I ought to have it checked out. That's when I started panicking because check-ups mean doctors and hospitals, and hospitals, for me, mean cancer and not coming back out. So I went to the doctor two days ago, and he just made things worse because he said I had to go to Castle Hill and maybe have a biopsy. I didn't even know what one was but it just sounded horrible, especially when all I wanted him to say was that everything was completely normal. Anyway, he booked me in to see Mr Fox who Mum sees for check-ups, so that made me feel a bit better.

Hospitals make me feel sick, though. They just remind me of Grandma at the end and now of Grandad. Since we got back from Florida he's been getting worse and has recently been diagnosed with bowel cancer. Think he might be going into Princess Royal hospital this week for his first lot of tests and treatment.

Mum and Dad both came with me to the hospital today which was pretty embarrassing, because Dad obviously knew what it was about but he's male and doesn't understand these kinds of things. Luckily it was only Mum that came inside with me. I had to go to the breast screening department and get changed into this paper-thin gown. When I went in to see Mr Fox I was really embarrassed because I was sure it was nothing and felt I was just wasting his time. I didn't know he would actually want to feel me. His hands were really cold against my body, and I felt a mixture of fear in case something was wrong and discomfort at my body being on display. I felt daft crying but when Mum held my hand I couldn't help it. Mr Fox told me it was necessary to do an ultrasound before the biopsy, and then I just couldn't stop crying. I'd thought that ultrasound was only for pregnant women, and was convinced by this point that something major was wrong. Two women did the ultrasound. The gel was cold and smelled weird. I breathed a huge sigh of relief when the female doctor said she couldn't see any signs of damaged tissue. Mr Fox said I still had to have the biopsy, though, and out came this huge needle; he stuck it all the way into my chest and drew out what looked like a mixture of blood, water and skin. It was gross. He told me it was only procedure and he was pretty sure nothing was seriously wrong, but I still couldn't stop crying as I left the room.

In the waiting room I felt like such an idiot, though. There were women sitting in that room who were obviously really sick. One girl was so thin and pale her tiny legs didn't look as though they would support her as she stood up. I stopped crying pretty quickly after that but I can't help feeling sorry for myself now. What if something is wrong with me? What if I'm back in that waiting room soon, in the same position as those other women? I get the results back in two to four weeks so I'll just have to wait until then to find out. I just hope to God everything's OK.

16 JULY 2003

T hank God. My hospital test results have come
back OK. We hadn't heard anything back from the
hospital so I rang the GP's surgery today and they said
the results showed everything to be completely normal.
I can't tell you how relieved I am. I'm totally happy
now.

Everything's going well at home, too. Rachel turned
eighteen in June and we had a big party at the house
for her. Loads of her friends came and I was allowed
to invite Abby round, so all in all it was a really good
night. Emma's got a place on a York uni scheme to go
to Norway for two months from January; she gets to
see what the education system is like over there for a
comparison study to primary education over here.
Pretty awesome but it's gonna be bloody freezing, and
Mum and Dad are planning on a January visit!
Kathryn's put us all to shame again by getting a place
at MIT in Boston for a year next year. It's like a

student exchange scheme; she moves across and studies medicine over there, including going to the Harvard medical school. I remember when we went to Canada, we also travelled down into the US and visited Boston and Harvard, and I told Dad how much I wanted to go there one day. Now she's gone and beaten me to it. Sometimes I wonder how I'm ever gonna make Mum and Dad proud of me when I have her for a sister; she makes me so jealous sometimes because she makes it all look so easy!

Speaking of Mum and Dad, they've gone away to a hotel in Warwickshire for their silver wedding anniversary. They're going to be away for a couple of days. I hope they have such a good time; they hardly ever get to spend time together. Dad got Mum the nicest present as well; Kathryn went with him to pick it out a couple of days ago. It's a white-gold heart on a chain with a diamond encrusted in it. He's probably been saving for it for months, but the money was worth it, he said, just to see the look on her face. He hid it in the back of the car as well so he could give it to her yesterday, which was the actual day of their anniversary. How cute is that? It reminded me of last Christmas when he made out he hadn't really bought Mum a Christmas present then handed over a Mariah Carey CD. The problem being that she hates Mariah Carey, and also that we hadn't got a family CD player to play it on anyway. She pointed this out and that's when Dad led her out to the car where the biggest family entertainment system was sitting in the boot. She still wanted to take the CD back, though!

When I watch them day to day I sometimes forget that they're a couple and about all the time they had together before we were even around. Deep down I think theirs is one of the strongest relationships I've seen. Their marriage as like a very durable metal; when the heat is on, things become slightly weaker, but the temperature has to get extremely hot before things will start to break down, and when other things are added to the mixture to test it, it simply comes out the other side stronger than ever before. They know each other so well they have started to finish each other's sentences, and they don't even have to ask how the other is feeling because they can tell from the sound of their voice or the look on their face. Despite everything they have gone through, I still think of my parents as being the strongest people I know and my personal heroes. I sometimes think that if we ever suffered a hurricane, once it had passed through and destroyed everything, my mum and dad would still be standing, clutching on to each other for survival.

This is making me a bit depressed about not having someone of my own to love. Still very fat and very friendless and, most of all, still very single. Oh, when will someone actually want to go out with me? Friends are still going down to the park in Beverley and hanging around with the older guys. Me and Abby aren't really talking at all, and she does everything with Michelle now. Mum says these things just happen and that I'll find another close friend soon enough, but for the minute I just have to look forward to what looks like a very uneventful and lonely summer.

17 JULY 2003

Got some really exciting post this morning and just had to get my diary out to write it all down. A few weeks ago we decided at one of the Madagascar meetings that we were going to hold a charity auction in the New Year. The plan was to write to loads of celebrities and companies asking them to donate things that we can auction. No one had a clue where we could start until someone found this thing called *The Star Directory*. It's basically a big phone book that lists the contact details for either celebrities themselves or the agents who represent them. You pay £6 for a page of this 'phone book' and then you're free to contact whoever takes your fancy on the page. We paid out the money to get a copy of a different page each and I got one with the end of the As, most of the Bs and a couple of Cs. Since then I've been sending off letters to the various celebrities on my list. Well, to cut a long story short, this morning a parcel arrived for me. It was a huge padded envelope which had a HMS prison stamp in the corner. When I opened it, a very heavy, leather-bound book tipped out onto the floor. Attached to the book was a cream letter from Jeffrey Archer! He'd sent me a signed, limited edition copy of a collection of his short stories and he'd sent it to me from prison! It's an amazing book, really beautiful, and I hope it gets a lot at the auction. I can add it to my collection anyway. So far I've received a signed pen from Tony Blair, signed photographs from Victoria and David Beckham, a signed CD from Norman Cook (aka Fat Boy Slim) and a signed wooden spoon from Jane Asher. It's so cool! At the school they've got loads more stuff, including signed Madonna things, a box of free stuff from Graham Norton, signed football shirts and photographs. Just yesterday someone got a film poster of *The Road to Perdition* signed by the director Sam Mendes.

I can't wait for the auction now; hopefully it will raise enough to cover the costs of our visas. Been training a fair bit the last few weeks. We're members at a health club, and even though you're not supposed to use the gym until you're sixteen Mum and Dad have been sneaking me in so I can try and get fit for the trip. I even suggested to Dad that if I can stay fit when I come back from Madagascar then we could go running together, and I might apply for the London Marathon when I'm eighteen. That may be pushing it a little bit, though. I mean, in the last cross-country run at school I only didn't come last because a girl had an asthma attack behind me and two other girls had decided to walk the entire course.

24 AUGUST 2003

The last few days have been a bit of a nightmare. Dad started getting down again last week after an audit in the office. Wednesday and Thursday were really bad days. He wouldn't go into work and just spent the day on the sofa, swiftly moving through phases of crying, shouting and sleeping. The rest of us are used to the routine that emerged, so we carried on as usual. Sometimes we cry – often when he refuses to talk to us or when Mum's been sobbing on our shoulder for an hour – but usually we just try to ignore him.

On Thursday afternoon we got him into the study, after a talk with my mum and Kathryn about the thing that was troubling him most: money. Kathryn decided that to help she would discuss with him a loan that was available to her as a medical student. She could apply for it because she didn't have the debts attached to her name that my parents did. After much persuasion from her, Dad agreed that yes, she could apply for it in order to help. I'm probably the only fifteen-year-old in Britain who is fully aware of their family's finances. And it is the kind of knowledge I do not wish on anyone. No one (no matter how old) wants to know that their father is thinking of sending the business into liquidation because it's not making much money. How do you respond when you're told that? 'Great, how wonderful. Do let me know when we're penniless.' No, I don't think so somehow, especially when your father is hunched over in his chair at one end of the table looking so pathetic you have this underlying need to go and shake him.

On Friday, after much huffing and puffing, immature stomping around the study and sulking, we got him to go into work. Those of us left in the house breathed a sigh of relief because although we knew he wasn't better it felt so much lighter in the house because the grey cloud had momentarily lifted.

On Friday night we had a family portrait session scheduled. It was part of a special offer Mum had seen in a supermarket. A full hour of smiling at a camera when five members of the family are feeling like they want to strangle the sixth, and the sixth could well be thinking of ways to strangle himself. But we went all the same, and we could tell he was trying. He tried to muster enthusiasm and although we all kept looking at each other, full of concern, he was responding when we spoke to him and appeared to be taking an interest in other people rather than wallowing in his own feelings.

It was a 'Venture' session where you just have this white room and you all have to do stupid things for the camera. We decided to all wear jeans and white tops, not really a good idea because we kind of blended in with the background, but it was fun anyway and it definitely cheered me and my sisters up when the photographer made Mum and Dad have photos taken of them kissing. Mum didn't seem to be much happier, though.

When we got back from the session Dad went straight back on the sofa and Mum wept upstairs. She told me that she didn't want us to live our lives around an illness. She hadn't envisaged her life to be like this, she said, and she never wanted it to be this way. I was firm with her. Sometimes I can just cry with her, but other times I feel angry because I know that there are so many people in the world worse off than us. I told her she should be glad that it is not like this all the time, that it's only occasionally, and that for the rest of the time we should consider ourselves lucky. She agreed, but I could tell she wasn't feeling too lucky right then.

On Saturday we had arranged to visit Rachel's university accommodation in Sheffield. We all went, although Dad slept all the way there and barely said a word all the way around. He later explained to my mum that he felt awful because it was like dangling a carrot in front of Rachel, knowing that he would only have to take it away if the money situation didn't improve. But he said later on to me that he felt he behaved badly by not showing an interest in where his child would be spending the next three or four years of her life. It's like he's some kind of Jekyll and Hyde figure, almost as if he's battling between the illness and the man it's forcing him to be, and his true self and the man he wants to be. I just wish he was one person all the time and not the pathetic figure he turns into when he's feeling low.

Today we had to take Kathryn to the airport so she could start her year in Boston. Dad seemed to be getting better. He got up. He took her cases to the car and drove part of the way there. He was quiet but that was expected; he tends to be a bit embarrassed when he's coming out of an episode. He was fine at the airport, but when she left we all cried, not only because we wouldn't see her for at least a few months but because we all knew how strong she had been for the past few days. She made him promise that there would be no more silly episodes from him but already, back at home, he has broken that promise and is back down in the depths of despair.

I really cannot cope with him. I just want him to pull himself together, and although I know it's not that easy, I don't know how much longer I can cope with this.

Going to the shop this afternoon for a loaf of bread was torture in itself. Mum made Dad come with me to get some fresh air. I would have preferred to just go there and back quickly. It is so hard being with him through that stage, the stage where he feels sorry for himself, the pathetic crying. He doesn't talk, and when he does utter something it's not about anything of significance. It's like walking with a coffin chained to your foot. It doesn't say a word but I know it's there, weighing me down, and I know what's inside is far from alive right now. That may seem harsh but it's true. For a time I feel sorry for him because I know it must be hard feeling so hopeless and desperate, but after a while, once I see him rest his head on his hand for the tenth time during a meal, it starts to annoy me and I get angry, not with him but with the nasty little fuck that's messing up his brain.

As if things weren't low enough for Dad right now, Auntie Liz rang with some news tonight of their father, Gramps to me. He's been hospitalised with liver problems and the doctors have predicted that he has a very small chance of living through the next month. Fucking typical. Bad things definitely come in threes in this house, if not sixes and sevens.

25 AUGUST 2003

Dad came into my room today and just said he wanted to let me know that he loved me. I didn't say it back. I was too angry with him. I explained that more than anything I needed him to try, just to try. He simply walked away from me like I was giving him a lecture he didn't want to hear. It's just so hard when you're baring your soul to someone and they are offering you nothing back. As Mum pointed out earlier today, we can deal with anything if we're together – moving house, working 24/7 – but what we cannot deal with is him giving up and not trying any more. Only when a person stops trying to succeed is he or she truly a failure. I wish I'd told him I loved him back, though, because, despite everything, I really do.

27 AUGUST 2003

He's such a bastard. A cruel, cruel bastard. It's Wednesday morning and Dad's gone missing. Just disappeared. My mum and I are on our own and he knows there's no one else here. He left a note on the message pad near the phone in the kitchen. It's nearly illegible but we could just make out what it said: 'Taking Missie for a walk and then going for a run. New leaf by me today!! Should be back b4 u anyway. X Rob.'

Nothing unusual about that, but when we had got home Missie was already back in the house. Normally he would take her with him for his run. I just don't know what he thinks he's doing. He took a key and left the door partly unlocked so he could get back in, yet it's been an hour and a half since we expected him back. We've been out looking but he's nowhere to be seen. How can he do this to us? When he's put us through so much in the last week alone, never mind the past fifteen years (of my life at least).

I often think, rather selfishly, why should I have to deal with all this crap? Then I think it's pretty normal for things to be shitty. Part of me knows that compared to some people I've got it easy. Millions of people are living in poverty, others are dying in squalid conditions, and even some of my closest friends have to deal with a parent's divorce or a split family, and I start to think I'm really lucky, but then I look at other people my age enjoying being fifteen, looking as though they don't have a care in the world, totally oblivious to any problems going on around them, and I find myself literally turning green with envy. He just makes me so angry.

I decided to write a diary entry mainly because I can't think of anything else to do. My sisters are all away and so there's no one to call. Mum says there's nothing we can do until he decides to come home or it's been long enough to call the police. It was so horrible coming back to the house, because it was like the other time, in October last year, when he wasn't answering the phone. But this time it was such a relief to see the Ford Fiesta still in the drive, and although Mum insisted she went into the house before me, there was nothing there, just the note. We were so relieved because it meant he was finally doing something, getting out there, but now that false hope has been snatched away.

False hope is the worst feeling in the world, worse than hate, worse than tension, worse than anything, because it gives you an illusion, lets you believe everything is going to be OK, and then all of a sudden that little tiny glimmer is snatched away from you and there is nothing again. Only it's worse than before the hope, because now it's twice as empty and you feel so much worse.

What can I do? I've gone out walking trying to see him, hoping he's hurt a knee or a foot and that he's not done this on purpose. I even saw an ambulance and a load of police cars under the bridge on the A63 and thought he might have stopped to help and lost track of time but really I know I'm just clutching at straws. What am I supposed to do next? I'm a fifteen-year-old girl looking for her 47-year-old father, who could be anywhere, doing anything. I have no hope, false or otherwise.

29 AUGUST 2003

This wasn't how it was supposed to be. I only ever wanted to write this diary to talk about our struggles and how, despite our problems, we were still so strong, how we were still a family. Not any more. Now I have to start a new phase to my diary and, really, a new phase to my life. Now every time I write about my father, my daddy, my protector, it will be in the past tense. I'll use words like 'was', 'used to' and 'did', because two days ago, on the morning of Wednesday, 27 August 2003, at precisely 7.40 a.m., my father died.

He glanced off the side of a lorry. He was wearing running clothes, had replaced his glasses with contact lenses, had our house key around his neck and had left the door on the latch as well as the note, telling us where he had gone. Yes, he was running on the side of a busy road. Yes, he had been down lately. Was it suicide? I cannot believe it was, but to be honest I can't be sure. That is something I will never ever know. I don't actually know which is worse: to think that he couldn't take it any more and had nowhere else to turn; or to think that after all this struggle, all these years of trying, of never giving up, that he had been snatched from us so cruelly. In my heart I have to believe that it was an accident. He left the note telling us he would be back soon; there was the key and the door on the latch. His behaviour was not unusual; he loved running. But the deciding factor was that he was feeling better. He had told my mum that morning, 'I am getting better slowly.' He would never normally go for a run unless he was feeling OK. If he was that black and down, he wouldn't have been able to leave the house. And besides, it wouldn't have been his style. He wouldn't have done something that would have risked other people's lives. Thankfully, no one else was hurt, but if he was going to do it to himself, to us, he would have chosen some other way, like the garage incident, or an overdose. He wouldn't have done it like that. Surely he wouldn't?

I miss him already. I cannot believe he's not coming back. I miss his hugs, the way the atmosphere changed when he walked into a room. I even miss his stupid loud sneezes. Mum's in complete shock but working on auto-pilot, moving round the house and going through the motions. It's just not right. They were soul-mates, meant for each other, two people who were supposed to grow old and grey together so they could travel the world.

Even just two days later, though, something else is gone from the house: the threat of his illness. It is like the death of a man who occasionally abuses. Except this was not physical, but emotional abuse, and that is one thing, the only thing, that stops after this. His life, and his memory, will live on in all of us, but the worrying and the depression stops here. I hope to God that he is happy now. I am not saying that this justifies his death or even eases the pain, because I would give everything to have him back, for him to be here with me now, hugging me and calling me precious, but I know only too well that if he hadn't been killed two days ago we could have lost him at any time in the future, and that wondering, that guessing when or how it would happen, is over. Mum keeps saying she's surprised he hasn't been taken before now. I think she thinks he did it, that he jumped out in front of the lorry. Oh God. I can't stop thinking about that moment.

When I first found out, the news ripped through me like a tornado, tearing at my insides. For the first hour after we'd heard the news, Mum didn't even cry. She phoned the police and then tried to calm me down. You see, we'd been out searching for him. It was about twenty minutes after I'd written my last diary entry and I'd persuaded Mum that we should go out looking for him in the car. At about ten to eleven we heard the news headline on BBC Radio Humberside; there had been an accident on the A63 that had caused major chaos. We waited in the car until the eleven o'clock news bulletin came on. It was the main story: 'There is a major hold-up on a main route into Hull this morning after a traffic accident at about 7.40 a.m. when a lorry hit a pedestrian. The dead man, who has not yet been identified, was believed to have been a jogger.'

We knew then that it was him. We got out of the car and went into the house. How on earth I managed to walk those few metres I will never know. We went into the house and I sat on the settee in the kitchen while Mum went to the phone. I walked around the kitchen screaming how unfair it was and how it couldn't be him. Mum had to explain to the police what he looked like and if he had any distinguishing marks on his body. She was so calm. After she put down the phone she came over to me and just held me in her arms. We cried together, me much louder than her, and she told me I had to be strong, I had to be brave, for her. We sat and talked for about half an hour, about him and how we were ever going to survive without him. She told me we had to, we had to live on and succeed for him; it's what he would have wanted. He wouldn't want us to sit around mourning for him, she said, moping around the house; he would have wanted us to go on and make him proud, in everything we did.

That is what I will do. I vow it now, that he will be so, so proud of me. I'm going to go back to school and study hard for those GCSEs. I'll get good grades and go on into sixth form so I can go on to university and get a good job. One day, I'll run the London Marathon. He won't be there, running alongside me, but I'm still going to do it, for him at least. I'm going to work hard, earn loads of money so my mum will be well looked after, just as he would have wanted. I will do so much, everything he will no longer be able to do, and he'll be watching over me, a smile on his face and a tear in his eye, so proud of his baby girl.

Mum and I had taken Emma and Rachel to the airport that morning for their girly holiday to Ibiza. Kathryn was in Boston. Mum had to tell them over the phone that their dad was dead, that he had been killed just metres from their house when they were thousands of miles away. That was the hardest thing for both of us. I could hear Emma crumble on the other end of the phone while Rachel screamed hysterically, yet I was unable to hug them, tell them everything was going to be OK. And Kathryn was on her own in a foreign country with strangers. We couldn't get hold of her until 7 p.m. that Wednesday night. She was devastated and blamed herself for not being here. A few days before she had gone, when Dad was really down, he had told Mum how he didn't want Kathryn to go away because her being there, her mere presence, made everything better. Mum told Kathryn this but of course she still went (knowing that it was the depression and the pathetic side of him talking). Now she curses herself for not staying behind, but, as I told her, even if the whole world had been here that day, no one could have stopped it. After being told the news she then had to endure a transatlantic flight home and then a five-hour drive from Heathrow. I went with Nick to pick her up, as Mum couldn't drive and had to be at home for Emma and Rachel.

Standing there, in the arrivals lounge, it felt so unreal. There were people around me laughing and glad to be home, and I was just standing at the railing, the bottom ripped out of my world. When I saw her, we just held each other for ages, in this sea of people and suitcases. The drive home was so long it was unbearable; I thought Kathryn was the strongest of us all and I'm sure, in time, she will be, but in the back of that car she was uncontrollable. Yet there is nothing I can say to make it better because she feels exactly the same way I do, with five more years of memories and pain.

It was only yesterday that the events of the day before began to sink in. On the Wednesday afternoon I had been to the mortuary, to see his body. The policeman, our so-called family liaison officer, drove us there. It seems harsh to slate the man for only doing his job but I don't think it's possible to like someone who's just told you the worst news in the world. (Not only that, but when he arrived at the house and we told him we already knew it was Dad, he replied something like, 'Well, at least that's the worst bit of my job over with then.') The mortuary was on a rough estate in Hull and as we travelled there we got lots of abuse from pedestrians, because we were in the rear of the police car. If only they knew. When we arrived, the door had to be unlocked from the inside, and a rather masculine woman appeared to greet us. I was asked repeatedly whether or not I wanted to see him. Ann, Mum's friend, was with us, and she asked if I had ever seen a dead body before. I hadn't but I thought to myself that it wasn't just a dead body; it was my dad. They told us he had multiple injuries to the head and the body, but that they would be covered and we could see his face. Also, he would be behind a glass screen so we couldn't touch him and I definitely couldn't hit him, which I felt so inclined to do at that moment. I felt so angry after the initial hysteria had passed. Not angry with him, I suppose, but angry that it had had happened and that he had left us behind.

A white sheet covered his body up to his neck and then swept around the face and over the top of his head. His left side faced us because the lorry had hit the right side. I went right up to the glass and touched it. If you could somehow block out the blood that stained his cheek and clotted between his lips, you could pretend that he was just asleep. His features were not out of place and the skin not badly marked. His eyes were closed and his long, dark eyelashes, which my sisters and I have all inherited, rested on his cheeks. He looked so peaceful, and just as he had been that morning when I had looked in on him before we left for the airport. I hadn't even said goodbye because I was angry with him for being down again. He had been fast asleep in bed, his head resting on the pillow.

It was partly a relief to see him at peace, free from the torment that had rattled his mind for the previous week and so many times before that. At last the suffering was over. The policeman said that his death would have been instant, that when the lorry hit him he would have felt no pain, just numbness as he was taken away. I'm glad of that at least.

Yesterday afternoon Mum and I went to the hospital to tell Grandad. He's been moved to Castle Hill from the nursing home for more tests and, basically, to make him comfortable before the end. The whole experience was horrible. We entered the ward and told the ward sister what devastating news we had for him. She drew the curtains around his bed and gave us some privacy. There is no way of telling someone easily; you just have to come out with it and wait for their reaction. Grandad's reaction was one of the worst. His face crumpled and I saw utter devastation in his eyes. Dad was like a son to him. Had he been well I doubt his reaction would have been much different but sitting there in that bed, NHS blankets up to his neck, I think I saw him give up, on everything. He didn't know what to say to console Mum and I. What could he say? While we had been trying to console ourselves that somehow everything could be OK, Grandad was honest and brutal and asked us, simply, how we were going to cope. In the past Grandad had always been there for Mum to talk to about Dad, a situation which even his own parents were unwilling to discuss, and now everything, all that advice and support, seemed to come crashing down around us. He was inconsolable, and looked more ill than I had ever seen him before. With hollow eyes in a yellowing face as his skin hung off what used to be his sturdy frame, he looked so lifeless. Sitting around his bed, everything that had gone before – this life that we had built for ourselves, a support network, a fragile framework that centred round Dad – seemed so pointless. Now that framework has collapsed, and we don't know what to do with ourselves.

I still cannot believe it. Today I've just been wandering around the house. There are so many people here but still it feels empty. I just want everything to stop. I had a bath tonight and just sat there crying for over an hour. Sinking underneath the water, I felt as if I didn't want to come back out. I would have been happy just to have been taken away, literally to drown away all my sorrows in the hot, soapy water.

For the last two nights I've slept in Mum's bed with Kathryn. Apparently I've been talking in my sleep, reassuring them over and over again that everything will be OK. I just wish I could believe it myself. I wake up and wonder if it's all been a dream. Sometimes I even forget it has happened, and think we're just waiting for him to come home from work. I don't know how I will get past these next few days. The vicar is coming round tomorrow to discuss the funeral but I'm not ready for that yet. Having a funeral means accepting that I have to say goodbye. How can I do that when all I want is my dad back?

30 AUGUST 2003

We had to venture into the study today, Dad's territory. Mum needed to find insurance documents and check that we were going to be OK financially. She pulled out a big brown metal box where all the important documents like passports and their wills were kept. With it we found a narrow brown envelope simply addressed to 'The Girls'. In the corner was the date, 15 July 2000, and a note that read 'ONLY open in the event of our deaths! X Dad'. Mum explained that when they had gone to Paris for their anniversary a few years earlier they had decided to write a letter to us explaining the procedure, should anything happen to them while they were away. The four of us opened it together in the lounge and Kathryn read it out. It was written, again, in his illegible scrawl with a blue biro on accounts paper. The first page was simply administration: who would have custody of us until Kathryn was eighteen, where we could find the life insurance policies, that kind of thing. He even managed to get a joke in about hopefully finding a lottery ticket on his person to improve the financial assets. The second page, however, was much more gut-wrenching. It read:

Now for the important stuff. I feel silly writing a 'goodbye just-in-case letter' but what the hell, here goes.

We've done our best (we think) and tried to impart values and love for each other, plus a work ethic. I've been very short-sighted and never done enough with my life in terms of giving happiness to others – there is very little of my 'misanthropy' in any of your genes and you all have enough ability and confidence to do and be anything you want. Do one thing only for me. Live life. Never have regrets.

Think of us from time to time. We will be there for you in your darkest hours, and hope these will be few and far between. Always be there for each other and value each other's opinions.

We love you to bits and are so, so proud of you. Go out and take the world by storm!

X Mum and Dad (x^{+1})

P.S. No black to be worn at our funeral. Take the dogs? Both to be cremated. Cut the costs!

The symbol after the signature and the kisses was that of the power of infinity. It was something Mum and Dad, both maths mad, had always written in Valentine's cards and letters to one another.

This letter in front of us meant so much. Whatever had happened on Wednesday, it showed he really did love us ridiculous amounts. It was as though I could hear him talking to us through the letter, and, as much as it hurt to read it, it was comforting to think he had thought about this eventuality, although obviously the letter was supposed to be from Mum as well.

I am so mixed up in my head. I feel lucky that I've had him for so long and am grateful for everything I still have from him, but at the same time angry and selfish because all I want is for everything to go back to how it was.

1 SEPTEMBER 2003

S till walking around in a daze. I've lost about half a stone, my eyes are black and hollow, and I feel as though I've lost all meaning to my life. I feel as though I'm dealing with it, and then the phone goes and it's another person ringing to give their condolences or a reporter wanting a quote for their story. There seems to be so many people to tell; the list is endless. There were people he had gone to school with, played rugby with, been in Junior Chamber with, worked with and dined with. There will be so, so many people who will mourn for him and yet, when he was down in the depths of despair, he could not see that he was surrounded by love, by people who thought he was an amazing person. If only he could have realised that. Would he still be here if he had?

We've received at least a hundred cards so far; they pour through the door every day. People say things like 'Rob was a bloody good egg', that he was 'a true gentleman', 'a father figure'. A man who went to primary school with Mum and Dad sent Mum an email and said how devastated she must be because, always, since the days of Rivington Primary, she had been 'Rob's girl'.

The most common message in the cards has been: 'What a shock. Rob was an amazing man, so kind and generous. He will be sadly missed.' He really will, and not just by us. I mean, he did some wonderful stuff. About six years ago he decided the town of Beverley wasn't festive enough and decided to organise a Christmas lights scheme where nearly every shop and restaurant in the town had a Christmas tree decorated with twinkling white lights. That year, and every year that followed, he made me and my sisters hand out leaflets advertising the scheme, and he spent the first and last week in December putting up and taking down trees. He was crazy sometimes, but that's what made him so special. There was the time he and a local bank manager dressed up as Rosie and Jim all day at work to raise money for a local charity, or the time he made us all travel up and down the country in a minibus as part of the 'Running Water' charity, raising awareness for Third World water shortages. Not to mention the four London Marathons he has run. I think that he did all this stuff because when he was well, back to normal, he felt selfish and ashamed that he had been so self-absorbed when he was down, and hadn't noticed how lucky he was and that there were so many others worse off than him. When he was ill it was as though he became enveloped in this big black cloud, and when the cloud lifted it was like being reborn and he got this sense of really being alive and was grateful for that life.

Even now, though, so soon after his death, I feel thankful for Dad's life. I know deep down that I'm lucky to have had him for as long as I have. Some people grow up never having a father figure. Mum is lucky that they had children together and that his memory can live on in the four of us and in his grandchildren, in particular the first boy born to one of us, who shall be called Robert. We're lucky we still have each other.

Today, three days before the funeral is due to be held, we had to go shopping for food for guests who would come back to the house after the service. All five of us went together, frightened to let anyone out of our sight in case they came to harm. Sainsbury's seemed such an unreal experience. Families were arguing in the aisles and we were shell-shocked, wandering through the scattered trolleys like deer caught in headlights. Price didn't matter; we just slammed things in the trolley that we thought we should buy. We were near the end of the shop when Mum remembered we should get some fruit juice, so Kathryn went off in search of it. A few minutes later she returned to us at the checkout, carton in hand. She held up the item she had picked. 'I thought this seemed appropriate,' she said. It was a carton of Five Alive. She held her breath as she waited for our reaction; luckily we all looked at each other and laughed. What else we could do?

This evening we went back to Venture. Mum is determined to buy some of the photos we had done. The viewing session was horrible. Seeing him there on a 6ft screen it's impossible to believe that he's no longer here. We chose the pictures we wanted, regardless of price. Somehow it felt very fateful that we'd had the photo session when we did; we'd been offered a later date but had refused it. If we'd accepted then Dad wouldn't have been here for it. Even though the night the photos were taken wasn't really a happy occasion, the pictures are now one of the few memories we have left of the six of us as a family, and that makes them invaluable.

3 SEPTEMBER 2003

We had to go into the office today. No one is really sure what will happen to the business yet. At the minute Dad's colleagues are avoiding going anywhere near the closed door of Dad's room, and are just keeping everything ticking over on a day-to-day basis. Half the cards we've had at home are from clients, so obviously no one is sending any work through.

His room was exactly how he would have left it. The window blinds were raised so that the view of St Mary's church was clearly visible from his chair. Dad used to take us there for midnight mass on Christmas Eve. It's a big church right in the centre of Beverley, old and beautiful but always overshadowed by the Minster at the other end of the town. Work lay in piles around the desk; there was a list in his scrawl entitled 'Things To Do Today'. His Eeyore business card holder sat miserably on the desk next to a heavy gold paperweight in the shape of the word 'DAD'.

A photograph of Mum lying on the beach in Cayman was propped up by a pot full of pens. Really old school photographs of my sisters and me were in a column on the wall behind his desk. There was his certificate of Junior Chamber Senator position and also his qualifications from the accounting body in England and Wales. Behind his desk hung a giant wall planner which included our birthdays and those of all his staff. I noticed he had pencilled in important meetings and dates throughout September. Today he was supposed to be a meeting with a client and an old friend.

Mum had brought a box with her to pack up his most personal belongings. She searched through all the drawers frantically as if she were looking for something. I think part of her believed that if he really did kill himself then he would have left some kind of message somewhere, a letter, note, or even an email. There was nothing. No indication that he didn't have the intention of returning to this office. Mum opened the middle drawer of the dark, heavy desk. There were Post-it notes, rubber bands, stamps, and, in the corner, two shiny pound coins that I knew were there for the next time I was fishing around in his drawer for some spare change to buy a 'Marathon' and some sweets. It made me really upset, seeing that money there. It was the smallest thing but it meant the world to me, knowing that it was there waiting for the next time I was in the office, whiling away the hours until he could take me home.

Take me home. Singing along to the radio, or talking about the stars. Stupid little things that made up our relationship. How I'd give anything to be able to walk outside now, see him unlock the passenger door of that big ugly car that I slated so much for being embarrassing. One more journey home, that's all I want, just one more half an hour with him.

5 SEPTEMBER 2003

The funeral was held yesterday. Mum had asked the vicar specifically not to have it on a Wednesday because I hated that day; everything bad seemed to happen on a Wednesday. The service was booked for twelve noon at St Mary's.

The funeral cars were due to arrive at half past eleven. By that time the house was already full of friends and relatives preparing for the buffet to be held afterwards. At eleven-thirty exactly the doorbell went. I answered it. Mum stood behind me. We were dressed in the customary black but I had pinned a small pink flower to my lapel. My hair was tied back in a half-pony, the way Dad liked it. (I'd worn it like that a couple of weeks earlier, at Kathryn's twenty-first and leaving do, where he had so proudly described me as the belle of the ball.) The man standing at the door reminded me of the cartoon character Beetlejuice. His grey hair was combed into a side parting and he was wearing black trousers with grey pinstripes, which narrowed at the bottom and tucked into his overgrown shoes. He offered his sympathy and asked if we were ready to go. Mum handed him the CD for the crematorium – 'Somewhere Over the Rainbow' by Eva Cassidy. I had wanted Simon and Garfunkel's 'Bridge Over Troubled Water' as it was a favourite of his, but when we listened to 'Somewhere Over the Rainbow' it seemed so perfect, especially the line 'where troubles melt like lemon drops away above the chimney tops'. That was what we'd always wanted for him, what he'd striven for, and we all hope, wherever he is now, that he has finally achieved a trouble-free existence.

My sisters, my mum and I climbed into the car. It was a beautiful car but there were six seats in the back and so there was one spare as we sat down. It's actually always the case – dinner sets, tables in restaurants, wine glasses – but you don't tend to notice until one of your special six is no longer there. That space seemed to glare at me throughout the whole journey. In the car behind sat Dad's sister, Auntie Liz, and her husband, my gran and my three sisters' boyfriends – Nick, Paul and Darren. They have been so strong during the past week. Poor Paul has only been going out with Emma for a week.

Arriving at the church was awful. My stomach did a back-flip as the car pulled up and I saw a sea of black standing outside the doors.

My legs were like jelly when we walked into the church, so much so that I tripped and fell down the steps, and was caught by Nick in front. I could not look up as I walked down the aisle, knowing that my friends would be standing there in support for me. Though I stared at the floor as I walked I could sense how full the church was. Every row was packed, the whole place full of people who had loved and respected my dad. We went to the front of the church and slipped into the first row of pews. As I was stumbling down the aisle I thought about the time I might next walk down the aisle of a church with all eyes on me and the fact that that day, at my wedding, he won't be there to give me away. I looked at my sisters and could tell their thoughts were pretty similar. What are we going to do without a dad?

The coffin was laid down on the props in front of us, and the one thing I noticed straight away was how small it looked, this wooden box, and I remember feeling horrified at the thought that they may have squashed him somehow to fit him in. My mum later reminded me that he was only a short man and that you shrink a tiny bit when you've died.

Weird to think that somehow it wasn't the same person in the box as the person who was alive and walking around just a week ago. That even his physical appearance would have changed, his organs taken out and rearranged during the post-mortem, his body dissected and sewn back up. The thought of it makes me feel sick. Kathryn and Emma chose to go to the funeral directors a couple of days ago to see him before they put him in the coffin. Without the protection of that sheet over his injuries I dreaded to think what state his face might have been in so I decided not to go with them. Kathryn said it helped to say goodbye to him properly and to touch him, even though what was there wasn't Dad. But Emma disagreed; she said his face was all contorted and squashed in on one side. Obviously the undertakers try to rectify the damage with their make-up and their tools, but it's not the same; she said there was no escaping the fact that he'd been hit by an articulated lorry at high speed. In other words, his face was fucked up.

The vicar started his speech when we were all seated. He started by welcoming everyone and then he said a short piece about my dad, what he did for a living and what kind of man he was. But as he was talking I couldn't help thinking that although what he was saying was not incorrect it wasn't enough. I wanted to run to the front and tell everyone of the battle he had every day, how he fought against a horrible illness and yet managed to keep it a secret from his friends and colleagues. I wanted to tell them about the fact that he never gave in, even on the darkest days. Yet I couldn't because they wouldn't understand, not really. And anyway, it was supposed to be a secret.

Kathryn got up to say a few words about him. I had wanted to say something but she felt it was 'right' for her to do it as she was the eldest. I was annoyed because I wanted to do him proud just as much as she did. But this is what she said:

I wanted to stand up here today and say a few words about my dad. But when I got to thinking about it I realised that the relationship that each of us had with him was so special and so individual that I could only ever hope to tell you what he means to me.

When I first started going out with Nick he used to say that ours was the only family he knew that stopped when my dad came home, and even at the age of twenty I was still running down the stairs to meet him and find out about his day.

I can't quite believe that he's never going to drive me down to Cambridge again, walk me down the aisle, tuck me into bed or call me his little girl any more.

My dad was an amazingly kind, generous and giving man, full of good advice, obscure knowledge and the occasional bad joke. I can't begin to put into words what he meant to me and I'll never know the relationships he had with each and every one of you. So, as I read this poem, I would ask you to think of all the memories you have of my dad and I ask God that hopefully, in our lives, my sisters and I can do him proud.

She then went on to read 'Death Is Nothing At All' by Henry Scott Holland. When she took her seat again there was not a dry eye in the church. At that moment I definitely felt she had done him proud. Although she cried nearly all the way through it, she was braver than I could ever have been.

As I climbed into the sleek car once more, this time to go to the crematorium in Cottingham, I watched the mourners leave the church. I saw a grown man, my dad's occasional running partner, emerge from a group of people, crying loudly and unashamedly. A large group of girls from my year, my school friends, were standing on the corner, all of them crying and hugging one another. At that moment I felt angry and so jealous. Yes they were upset and yes they were entitled to be, but when they got home that evening their lives would be no different; their dads would still be there for the goodnight kiss, and a bottomless pit would not have swallowed their stomachs like it had mine. I felt cheated.

We arrived at the crematorium, somewhere I'd never been before. It was set in beautiful surroundings and the building itself was very pretty, the front having a huge stained-glass window that overlooked the countryside. The inside was just like a church, with huge pews for us and the selection of other relatives who had accompanied us for the cremation. As we walked in, the music started up, Eva Cassidy's beautiful voice piercing the atmosphere, and that was it for me for the rest of the service. I could not stop the tears from running down my face. The music was loud and clear, and it sharpened every raw nerve in my body. The pit in my stomach got deeper, and it really dawned on me then that he was never coming back. He was gone for ever.

The vicar said a few words and blessed the body, then he flicked a switch next to him and the whirring noise started up as the curtains around the coffin began to close. Rachel turned to me and just held me while we sobbed to each other. Darren hugged us both from behind.

We had asked to keep the flowers that we had placed on top of the coffin because with them were some cards we'd written, our own personal goodbyes. Mine read: 'To my hero. You gave me so much in so many different ways. You will live on in so many people's hearts. Carry on watching, Daddy, because I'm going to make you so proud of your baby girl. Love forever. Sarah xxx'

My sisters had also, in their own ways, expressed what he had meant to them. Rachel called him her running partner. Emma said he was one of her best friends. Kathryn simply said he was everything she wanted the father of her own children to be, and more. Mum said she couldn't put down in words the conversation she wanted to have with him. Instead she had written: 'My darling Rob, No words can express how I feel. You were always there and now you've gone. I'll look after our four daughters until we are together again. Carol (xx)'

It made me realise I'm never going to know how she feels.

In the car on the way back to the house we all told each other how we didn't want to go inside and face all those people, but Mum told us we had to go in and do it for Dad. So we did.

There were hoards of people sitting in the lounge and even more people standing outside. I couldn't be bothered with small talk so I went and found my friends. Emma and Kaye were among the friends who had come back to the house as well as two girls I'd known since I was about two, Emma G. and Becca C. Each one of them gave me a hug of true friendship. It meant a lot them being there that day, as I didn't have to talk about my dad, about what happened, or the pain I was feeling.

Half the people there I didn't know anyway, and a lot of people didn't know me. A strange woman washing up in the kitchen took my plate from me after the buffet and instructed me where to put my rubbish; she actually told me where to find the bin in my own kitchen. That made me feel awful, I don't know why. Probably because I felt I had some sort of right for everyone to know who I was. I wanted to announce my grief to the world, to scream that although they missed him too, it was my daddy I'd lost. I felt people should be aware of me, and know what I was going through. I had this amazing sense of importance – although maybe that's the wrong word because I didn't believe I was important, but I had this feeling that everyone should know what had happened, every single little detail.

The feeling had been the same in Beverley a few days ago. Kathryn and I were walking through the town centre and we described to each other this feeling, the idea that we should tell everyone passing us of our loss. It reminded me of a poem that had been on the front of a card someone had sent us. It's called 'Funeral Blues' by W.H. Auden and begins:

Stop all the clocks, cut off the telephone.
Prevent the dog from barking with a juicy bone.
Silence the pianos and with muffled drum,
Bring out the coffin, let the mourners come.

That was exactly how we felt, that because our lives had been interrupted in such a way everything else should stop, too. We were completely engulfed in our own feelings. It didn't seem fair to us that other people should be able to carry on with their own lives undisturbed while we had this great thing to deal with. It just wasn't right but, as you're always told when you're younger, life isn't fair. God knows I've learned that in the last week alone.

6 SEPTEMBER 2003

Gramps, Dad's dad, died last night. Liver failure. Half of me doesn't even care, and part of me thinks it serves him right, as, like many old men, he liked a whisky every so often. Then the other half feels ripped apart once more by grief and emptiness. In less than a week Auntie Liz has lost a brother and a father, and Gran a husband and a son. We're not going to the funeral. Since they moved up to Scotland a couple of years ago we've not seen a lot of them and we've got enough to deal with already. Shit. This has been the worst week of my life.

9 SEPTEMBER 2003

I had to go back to school yesterday, less than two weeks after Dad died. Mum and I had agreed to go back on the same day, to face it together, but at different schools. Kathryn has gone back to Boston. It seems as though we just have to move on. Mum only took a week off work. Some people said she wasn't ready to go back but she argued it was what she needed, some kind of routine to get into.

I walked back into school not knowing what to expect. I had only spoken to a few of my friends since it happened and had asked them to spread the word, but I didn't know how far 'the word' had spread and how people had reacted. Did they care? Would they be suspicious about the circumstances in which Dad had died? I wasn't thinking how I felt. I was just concerned about how other people would react to me.

I was right to be concerned. As I walked into my form room it kind of went quiet, leaving just a few people talking loudly. Emma and Kaye sheltered me. I tried to make conversation about other subjects, light-hearted things that wouldn't have any relevance, but as I did I couldn't ignore Abby and Jess sitting at the end of the row, whispering together, trying their best to avoid even looking at me. I hadn't spoken to them all summer. Was it naive of me to think they would forgive me for not seeing or talking to them consider-ing the shit I had been through? Obviously it was. I'd thought that everything that had happened before could have been forgotten, that maybe they'd be there for me after everything that had happened. But they just didn't seem to know how to respond to me. It was as if the gap that had grown between us has been made ten times larger over the summer. Maybe it's now too big to be repaired.

Thankfully not everyone was so insensitive. Many people throughout the day just came up to me and wrapped their arms around me, hugging me. That was nice. And then there were the teachers. I don't know if Mrs Hill felt she was doing good by standing in front of my whole form and asking to speak to me, but she did it anyway, and I think she found it hard to not hug me herself. She had been one of Dad's clients and wanted to know how I was. I didn't know if this was a normal thing for a teacher to do in this situation. She asked me if I wanted all my other teachers to know. I said yes, even though I wasn't sure what effect it would have. It seems that the effect had been huge. So far, in just two days, I've been given at least fifteen cards and letters from members of staff at my school. Some just expressed sincerest condolences; others took the time to write about just how much my sisters and I meant to them and how deeply shocked and sorry they were for our loss. 'Loss' – it's such a stupid word. It makes it sound as though we've just misplaced him.

School is so surreal, like another world, one where I don't belong. I feel I should be in a desolate landscape where there is no time and no people, only emptiness and a feeling of eternity. Instead I'm back in this world of routine and normality, but I don't know what's normal and what's not any more. People look at me like I'm lost, and, in a way, I think I am. I can see them judging me, but deep down do I really care? When you start to consider other people's perception of you, you wonder how much they know or even how much of what you tell them they actually believe.

I've always been someone who is quite conscious of what other people think of me and how I am viewed, and have lied horrendously to cover up any goings-on at home. My sisters were the same, so much so that, because of the impression we gave of our home life, some people at school began to call us the Waltons or Swiss Family Robinson. We were told by many that we had the perfect family life. I used to disagree and even get angry at such comments but now I've thought about it, we did have a very good family life, despite our problems. I wouldn't go as far to say it was perfect because I don't know the meaning of that word, but we loved each other and that's what matters. Every family has their differences and their issues, but the thing that makes a successful family, a perfect family if you like, is the choices you make. You make the choice to stick it out instead of giving in when you fall at the first hurdle. You learn to love your partner and your children, you trust them and tell them your feelings, and you vow that whatever happens, whatever problems you have to face, you'll face them together.

But when Rachel and Emma go to their universities, we're no longer going to be together in the same house. Maybe that's why I'm feeling so adrift. Previously I knew who I was and where I belonged; I'm not so sure any more.

23 SEPTEMBER 2003

Somehow we've slipped into an uneasy routine. Emma has gone back to York and Rachel started at Sheffield Hallam last weekend. We dropped her off with all her things but after a while just had to leave her there, crying and alone. She seems to be doing OK after the first week; they have something called Freshers where you can meet lots of other people, and I think that must have made it a bit easier. Mum and I, on the other hand, have been taken into order by the school timetable.

An old client of Dad's drives me to school in the morning. I spend the day mindlessly at school and then undertake any extracurricular activities afterwards. If I have nothing planned I'll hang around town or go to the library and do schoolwork until Mum can come and pick me up. Sometimes I make the hour-long train journey and she picks me up at the station. Then we return home together and the long nights begin.

We make our tea as soon as we arrive home, stay together in the kitchen, eat and then tidy away. We then move to the study where I work on the computer, or chat about mindless topics on MSN messenger, and Mum works at her desk. At about eleven we both go upstairs to our rooms, drawing all the curtains and turning out the lights. We're trying to restrict our movements to five main rooms of our huge house, as if by moving elsewhere we would disturb something. We've even attached a small light to Missie so we don't have to go out into the dark garden to find her, scared that her shadow and wagging tail might turn out to be something more sinister. The house seems so big and empty; our feeble attempts to fill it by turning on all the lights and leaving the TV on are useless. After the first few times I became annoyed with Mum leaving the TV to play to an empty room so I've started turning it off, but the silence irritates her so she just refills the void with music from the CD player, or the tapping of the keyboard, or she'll open windows to hear the traffic drive by.

As I go to bed at night I'm tempted to leave my bedside lamp on, but I can never sleep with it on so I turn it off and, as I do, my bedroom comes alive. The dark wooden wardrobe is transformed into a coffin. Tall, dark and heavy, it seems to lurch forward, and sometimes, when I forget to shut it properly, the door swings open and causes me to catch my breath. I face the wall and then become convinced someone's standing over my bed, ready to attack as soon as I turn back round. When I face into the darkness of my room I can see Dad walking towards me, yet instead of being happy I'm terrified as he comes closer. I don't want him to touch me, am scared of seeing his face close up. Most nights I just persevere and, after a while, the visions go away; if they didn't I would just fall asleep through sheer exhaustion.

The worst nights are when the roads are quiet. Then, every so often, a lorry rumbles past and I begin thinking. The thoughts and images that come into my head are worse than any I see in my room. Every time I hear those lorries I view the impact. I see the blood as it splashes along the side of the vehicle; I see the mangled body being thrown onto the grass verge, Dad's face contorted in pain and fear. I envisage that accident from every single possible angle – from behind him, from the wheel, from under the truck, from the footbridge and sometimes from Dad's view. On those nights I have to leave my room. I run down the corridor, through Mum's door and into the empty side of the bed, where, if I inhale deeply into the pillow, I can still smell Dad's aftershave.

This is the life we are becoming used to, this kind of half-life, which I know, with time, will get easier. Or at least that's what everyone says. I just hope it happens soon.

2 OCTOBER 2003

It didn't get better. Instead it got a whole fucking lot worse. God obviously does not like us.

Grandad died on Friday evening. I didn't find out until Sunday, as I was staying over at Emma G.'s house – we'd been doing preparation for our Bronze Duke of Edinburgh expedition – and Mum didn't think there was any point telling me straight away. After all, he was dead. Not like there's anything I can do about it, is there? Death's pretty final. I should know because people just keep on dying on me.

Mum said she could see a change in him once he'd been moved to the nursing home in August, that he just stopped fighting. The nurses told us he died in his sleep. I went to see him a few days before and I just wish I'd been a bit more considerate. There he was, unable even to tell someone when he needed the toilet, and all I wanted to do was leave because the nursing home smelled of urine and stale food. He was grieving just as I was, and yet I couldn't even bring myself to have a proper chat with him because I was so wrapped up in myself. He looked awful that day; he didn't really know we were there either. He wasn't talking any sense and Mum got upset because I think she knew deep down it was coming to an end.

I remember seeing Grandma like that, a few weeks before she died in the summer of 1997. She had been to visit our house before we went on a camping trip, and she died the first night we were away. She had to drink through a straw and her skin had become a sunken grey colour, her stomach and limbs bloated. Cancer is the most horrible disease. Mum's been through it three times now. She told me that when Auntie Susan was at her lowest point, just days before she died, she stood up on the bed and sang 'Crazy' by Patsy Cline all the way through. I can't even begin to imagine the stuff Mum has been through. Widowed and orphaned within a month. I can't see how she can go on from here. I'm finding it difficult enough but she's got a lifetime of memories to come to grips with. How do you even start to handle it?

The funeral was held yesterday. It was at the crematorium in Cottingham again but this time there was no church service before. It seemed so odd and so unfair to be back there again so soon. Some people never have to deal with crap like this. Mum's had to cope with so much and still she manages to stay positive. She pointed out in her speech at the funeral that when she was twenty-one and had just got engaged to Dad, she could not even begin to imagine that at the age of forty-eight she would have said goodbye to the four most important people in her life at that time. It's the kind of loss I cannot even begin to comprehend, I who, in my short life, have been to four funerals and been in the funeral car for three of them. But despite her loss and aching, my mother, who is now my whole world, still found it in her heart to be grateful for those she still had with her. She said how, although she had lost those four people who meant so much to her, all four of them, in their own way, had helped her gain four more amazing people, her daughters, those that were left behind.

I can't help but marvel at her. I'm finding it hard enough to deal with the death of just one person, yet she still finds strength to carry on, to keep getting up in the morning and not giving up. When I ask her about it she says that it could be worse and that she is just used to it, this sense of routine, of carrying on when everything seems to be going wrong around you. At first I didn't understand what she meant and then I realised. She's lived with my dad's illness since he was diagnosed. By the time of his death Mum had perfected the art of pretending everything was OK to the judging public, continuing with everyday tasks while, inside the family home and inside her head, everything was so wrong and so mixed up. She worried constantly but throughout her life she has only confided in a small number of people – her close family and a few friends. All those other people who knew her and thought she was an amazing person for juggling a full-time teaching career with having four children had no idea of the other things she also coped with. But I don't want her to have to pretend any more. I want her to be able to break down and for me to be able to pick her back up again. She needs to grieve and expose herself to this horrible pain that engulfs every single bit of your insides.

A prayer was read out at the service yesterday; there were similar messages in many of the sympathy cards we've received. The words seemed empty to me. How can God exist when things like this keep happening? Mum says that when Auntie Susan died her faith in God was questioned, but she's since realised that things are sent to test you, and what doesn't kill you simply makes you stronger. It's the same old cliché but is it really true? Is there really this powerful force that does evil things simply to test our faith in him? To me it all sounds like complete shit. I was christened, I go to church once a year, I went through the whole Girl Guide thing and in junior school I was the one who knew the Lord's Prayer by heart. But is any of this actually real? I honestly think that God is just an easy way out; it gives us answers to a world that we otherwise wouldn't be able to explain. Deaths happen and people say God is testing our strength and our faith. Natural disasters happen and people say God is either punishing the world or cleansing it of its evils. Christians can find an answer to anything. Is it part of human nature not to like leaving things unexplained? I think we're just too scared of the unknown, too scared of waiting to find out what happens when we die. Isn't that just what heaven's all about? Knowing that there is somewhere good to go when it all turns sour on earth? I mean, if we couldn't explain away all the horrible things in the world there would be a lot of confused people around. After all, if there are no reasons, no explanations, then what is the point? Is there one?

I really don't have any answers; I have no idea what I believe. I think it's a nice idea. I'd love there to be a big guy with a grey beard up there looking out for me. I just think that if there is he's not really doing a very good job of it, and if it's my faith that he's testing then I've failed big time. As for my strength, at the minute I don't think I could face life out of bed never mind life in the real world.

I think about it a lot, though, this whole God idea. Part of me thinks if the big bang theory is true then someone had to have created all the tiny particles of matter in the first place. But then if God does exist, who made him? Things just don't appear. I'm too much of a believer in science not to know that. But that's about as far as my thoughts go. Maybe when I'm older I'll find an answer or an answer will find me. Dad wasn't confirmed until he was thirty-three; maybe God came and found him.

We got a letter from Macmillan Cancer Relief today. Instead of flowers at Dad's funeral we asked for donations. So far we've raised £1,214 for palliative care in the East Riding of Yorkshire. At least one good thing has come out of this. If only some of it could have gone towards Grandad's treatment, we might have had him for that little bit longer.

16 OCTOBER 2003

M um and I have had enough. Our routine has become too much to bear. Mum put the house on the market today and we've already started looking at houses in Beverley. In Dad's words, it's time for a new leaf.

30 OCTOBER 2003

It is a year to the day since we came home to find Dad sitting in our Ford Fiesta in the garage. What a lot has happened in that short space of time. I feel that my life has been totally altered and that I am in fact a completely different person. But now we have a house move and a holiday to look forward to.

We've found a new home in Norwood, close to the town centre in Beverley. It's not huge and is a simple end-of-terrace townhouse with enough bedrooms, a bathroom, kitchen and dining room, but it will only be Mum and I living there so it is all we need. It's close to town and a two-minute walk to school, and for the first time since Dad died I'm feeling excited about something. It's the best possible idea because here, in this huge rambling house, everywhere I look there are reminders of him. Not that I want to remove the aspects of him that remain here but having them around us 24/7 in this house that he chose and adored is too difficult. In Beverley we can make our own mark on the house and create new memories, just the five of us. We move in at the beginning of January, a new start for the New Year.

As for the holiday, it was only decided a couple of days ago. We were driving home when we passed the travel agents in Brough, and Mum decided that we should go on holiday for Christmas to avoid the pain of spending an empty Christmas at home. It was pure impulse, and partly because some of the life insurance money had just come through. She told the agent that she wanted a holiday in the Caribbean for five over Christmas and that money was no issue. The first holiday the agent found was in Antigua for two weeks and cost £15,000, which reminded Mum of her senses and that perhaps money was indeed a bit of an issue. We eventually decided on an all-inclusive in Barbados, not quite £15,000 but at the same time, not cheap. I couldn't believe it. Barbados for Christmas. Dad would have thought we were insane; the other three definitely thought so when I phoned and told them. We leave on 19 December, two days after my sixteenth birthday, and return just before New Year. I'm so glad we're going. Hopefully it will give us time to sort ourselves out and reaffirm the fact that we will be OK, despite everything that's happened.

30 NOVEMBER 2003

Mum sent out her Christmas cards today. A bit early, you might think, but she wanted to have them delivered before any started flapping through our letterbox. It has always been a tradition between Mum and Dad's long-distance friends to send newsletters at Christmas telling of each family's achievements that year. You know the kind of thing I mean – Fred and Jane Smith who we've met once in passing since Fred played rugby with Dad in the late 1970s. The family travelled to Bermuda in spring and cruised through the Norwegian fjords during summer and then little Sally and Peter were sheep in the Christmas play. Fred got a promotion so now the family can buy a new car and go on more holidays. It was that kind of exciting news. I think when they get our news this year it will be a little more jaw-dropping than most what-we-did-this-year newsletters. To those that already knew she simply sent a Christmas card. To others, those further afield who might not have heard the news, she enclosed a cutting from the Institute of Chartered Accountants local *News Review*, which described Dad's death as 'sudden and tragic'. Well, it's definitely sudden to receive that kind of news in your Christmas greetings. Kind of puts a bit of a downer on the whole festive season, doesn't it?

Anyway, I'm sure it'll mean another influx of sympathy cards. They're still arriving but the pace has definitely slowed down somewhat; I'd say we're down to getting two or three a week now. The ones we received in the first few weeks have been filed into a giant black box and split into sections; family, Dad's friends, Mum's friends, family friends. There's also a black file that holds all the letters and cards from the flowers that we received, plus the CD that was played at the crematorium. Is that weird and depressing? It seemed wrong just to throw them all away. I'd say we've got at least six hundred so far and still they keep coming. It's as if we're numb to them now; they just go in a pile and then get filed away. I can't wait for the day when the last card comes through the letterbox. Maybe then we'll be able to close the black box and move on. Barbados in nineteen days. Not long now.

7 DECEMBER 2003

J ust got home. Have spent the whole weekend at Safeway, packing customers' bags in the hope that they'll toss some loose change into our green buckets so I can be one step closer to getting on a plane to Madagascar next summer. Our last meeting was held in early September so I didn't make it. At the meeting they decided that for our first week we are going to visit an orphanage just outside the city centre. Thinking about doing things like that makes it all seem so much more real.

After everything that's happened this year I can't quite believe that I'm still going. Well, as long as I raise the money. I haven't been doing much fundraising for the last couple of months – I've been too lost in my own head – but I really have to get focused if I want to do this, and I really, really do want to do this. Just to prove that I can. Being out there today has made me really determined again. People asked what we were raising money for and why we were wearing ridiculously huge T-shirts emblazoned with the World Challenge Expeditions logo. Once we explained what we were going out there to do, remembering to get in the words 'orphanage' and 'Third World country', they would be emptying their spare coins in an instant. A quick guilt trip always works, although I was very festive this weekend and always made sure I said Merry Christmas, whether they gave me any money or not. Though I have to admit, the thought of being in Barbados in a couple of weeks makes it slightly easier to feel cheerful at the moment. I've nearly raised £1,500 for Madagascar but I still have £2,000 to go and only six months in which to raise it.

The planning for the New Year auction is going well, too; it's going to be held at the school in January. There's going to be a real auctioneer taking the biddings and refreshments sold before and after. We're selling programmes for £5 each, which entitles two people to entry and also lists all the things we have up for auction.

The Safeway I was at today is across the road from school and just five minutes walk from our new house. I can't wait to move. Still having nightmares. The sooner we leave Elloughton the better.

2 JANUARY 2004

I look in the mirror at my tanned face, inspect my newly manicured hands (completed pool-side by the in-hotel beautician) and can see the stacks of washing overflowing out of my suitcase onto the floor. Yet somehow I don't feel as though I've just come back from holiday.

My first glimpse of Barbados was through the tiny plastic windows of the plane as it touched down. Straight away I could see that it was a beautiful place. As I came down the steps onto the tarmac, the heat literally smacked me in the face. Even in December the weather was ridiculously enviable. We got a private transfer from the airport to the hotel.

The plain cream building (decorated with tasteful tiny fairy lights) was everything we could have wanted, and our rooms looked onto the beach and out over the sea. Across the road from the main hotel was a luxurious spa and second pool, the two being split by the main road that encircled the island. Standing on the beach you could see that the golden sands stretched for miles, accompanied by the crystal-clear turquoise waters, which kissed the shore every time a wave broke. Along the beach from our hotel was Sandy Lane, the infamous celebrity getaway hotel. It was rumoured that at the time two Hollywood stars and a music mogul were in residence there. In between that luxury accommodation and our hotel were dotted several more daunting mansions. Their cream exteriors shone in the sunlight and screamed power and money. Squeezed in between each residence were several shanty houses. Their tin roofs also shone in the sunlight, but with the reddish tinge of rust and the gleam of sewage hanging in the poor drainage system. We found out a few days later that the people who lived in these makeshift houses were offered millions of dollars for the plot on which they lived. Yet they adored the view and their location so much that they refused every single time.

A few hours after we'd arrived – when we'd had a look around, returned to our rooms and unpacked our things – we were sitting downstairs, surrounded by palm trees and being served tropical cocktails, but we still didn't quite know what to do with ourselves. It was as if we were scared of relaxing and enjoying the hotel because we felt the only reason we were there (and could afford to be there) was because of Dad's death.

The whole holiday passed in a similar fashion. Every single time we began to enjoy ourselves something would remind us of Dad, and we would fall back into our dejection once more. Every day was pretty much the same. We would rise early, go down to breakfast (which held an amazingly unique choice each morning), then head to the beach or the pool and lie on sunloungers until lunchtime, when we'd come inside for another buffet before returning to the beach or the pool for the afternoon. Then, each night, we would make our way upstairs, bathe and change and come back down for dinner. We'd make a fuss out of which cocktail to have (not that it mattered because they were all free and contained copious amounts of alcohol) and then we'd sit down at our (six-seated) table and have dinner. This usually occurred quite early (purely because there was nothing to wait around for), which meant that we were usually done and ready for bed by about half past nine. We were normally all filled with alcohol at this point. Somehow when I got the opportunity to drink it always seemed like a good idea. I know they say drinking is a depressant, but it is also a welcome distraction from whatever else is going on around you. Nobody ever really felt like talking after a meal because it was always the same topics that came up, and usually resulted in somebody being in tears.

It wasn't all routine and upset, though. On a couple of days we went shopping, another day we hired jet-skis, and, towards the end of the holiday, we took a Jeep tour around the island. That day started off very well. The driver (Charles) picked us up in the morning and we jumped in the back of the roofless 4 × 4 alongside another family and a Canadian couple.

We were taken on a tour through Barbados's main towns, through the sugar plantations and across each of the island's eleven parishes, which are each named after a different saint. The only female saint (which, by the way, is the highest point and looks down at all the other parishes) is called Lucy. We then drove up to a peak that overlooks the whole of the west coast. At this point Charles decided it was time for a break and stopped the jeep, taking out a huge keg of rum punch from the boot. We were all sitting around, just chatting and getting to know each other with a (very strong) glass of rum punch in hand, when Charles decided he would come over to talk to us. He asked why such a lovely group of ladies was holidaying alone and where the man of the family was. Of all the questions he could have asked, this was most definitely the worst. Mum simply told him that Dad was dead, killed in an accident three months ago. I think if Charles could have been engulfed by the nearest palm tree at that minute he would have been happy. The look on his face was one of pure shock and a classic foot-in-it expression.

He hardly made things any better for himself, though. As we climbed back on board he took the opportunity to wish 'de lovely family of ladeees' his 'most sincerest condolences'. Thanks, Charles. This resulted in more questioning from our fellow passengers, and for the remainder of the outing we all received sympathetic glances from whichever irritating person was sitting opposite us. I wondered if it was just Dad's way of making sure we were still thinking about him!

The jeep tour was about the most adventurous thing we did throughout our entire trip. Kathryn and Emma were planning a scuba-diving expedition, but Mum became convinced some ghastly end was going to meet them at the bottom of the ocean and persuaded them not to do it. So, pretty much every day we baked in the sun and drank rum cocktails from the 'rum shack' situated next to the hotel. It was no wonder that after a few days both Kathryn and Emma were suffering from sunstroke.

One day, in an attempt to protect me from a similar fate, Mum began an emotional battle with a parasol. She slowly struggled to open it fully and secure it with the plastic clasp, yet it slowly closed back up and sunk rapidly into the warm sand. After it collapsed for the fourth time she gave up and collapsed in a similar heap onto her sunlounger in floods of tears, saying that if Dad were here, he could do it. We all nodded in agreement and consoled her. It was Christmas Eve and, despite the subtle decorations in the trees and the not-so-subtle children's choir singing carols around the pool, it couldn't have felt further away from 25 December if it were the middle of June. It wasn't just the hot weather, though. We just couldn't muster any festive enthusiasm. That's probably why, on Christmas Day, like every other day, we were in bed by 10 p.m.

However, now that I've returned home I can appreciate that the holiday did in fact do as we'd planned. We spent Christmas together, away from any painful reminders at home, we relaxed and recuperated, and we returned home with a better outlook for the New Year. Let's just hope this year is going to be an improvement on the last one. Let's face it, it could hardly get much worse.

We move into the new house in less than a week. We will be leaving the house in Elloughton literally standing cold and empty, exactly how it seems just now. I have no regrets about leaving this cursed place. I simply hope whoever does end up buying it has better luck than we've had here.

12 JANUARY 2004

L ess than a week in our new house and already a death to christen the place. Max died early this morning. He was twelve years old; that's about eighty-four in dog years. It was strange; as he was sitting in his basket, fighting to get his breath, it reminded me of Grandad and his struggle towards the end.

I was lying in bed around midnight trying to get some sleep, when I first realised something was wrong. I heard Max whining and growling slowly in a really low tone, over and over again. Not wanting to wake Mum, I shuffled quietly down the stairs to see what was wrong. Max was padding up and down the kitchen floor, literally huffing and puffing like an old man. I could tell something was wrong but wasn't sure what it was. Missie knew, too. She was sitting quietly in the corner, her black fur resting against the kitchen cupboard doors. I opened the back door thinking he might be a bit sick and need to go outside. He struggled to get over the step and then, as he stepped onto the concrete, his back legs gave way. This was repeated a few times: up, shuffle, collapse; up, shuffle, collapse. I eventually coaxed him back inside and into his basket where I tried to get him to drink some water. Finding his water bowl empty, I refilled it and watched as he lapped up the contents in seconds. This happened twice more; his thirst seemed to be never-ending. Then, all of a sudden, constant dribble poured from his mouth, and foam seemed to appear through his wet brown nose. I knew then that something was seriously wrong.

Running up the stairs to get Mum, I was crying already. Max had been around since I could remember. When he was a puppy I'd try to crawl onto his back for 'horsey-rides' around the house. Mum came down straight away, just as concerned as I was. By this time Max was making strange hiccupping noises, as if he needed to be sick. It sounds impossible but his golden fur was slowly turning a faint green colour and since I had left him just a few moments earlier his stomach had started to swell. I tried my best to make him comfortable while Mum tried to get hold of the emergency vet. His breathing was becoming more and more rapid and his stomach more and more bloated. It was another hour or so before the vet arrived, by which time Max was obviously in considerable pain. His big brown eyes had widened to what seemed like twice their size, almost as if he were appealing to us to help him.

The vet knew straight away what was wrong. It turned out he had gastroenteritis, basically brought about by the fact that dogs can't burp like humans can.

He had a build-up of trapped air in his stomach which was fuelling breeding bacteria and worsening the virus. The vet said we could either wait until he died slowly and naturally, or we could choose to have him put down. To be humane we chose the latter.

Missie didn't like the vet going near Max, and so we had to take her out of the room while the lethal injection was administered. Afterwards she was allowed to go back in to say goodbye; apparently if she knew he was dead then she wouldn't pine for him after the vet took him away. She wasn't sure at first, though, and kept nudging his nose with hers, trying to get him to wake up. After that didn't work she curled up next to him and rested her little head on his now huge stomach. After a few minutes she realised something was wrong and started whining and barking at him. The vet then wrapped Max up in a blanket and carried him to the boot of his Land Rover.

It was about 4 a.m. when I eventually got back to bed, but there wasn't much point; I was crying too much to sleep. This morning it seems ridiculous to have cried so much over a dog. Yet Max represented part of a life that seems to be fast evaporating, taking everyone and everything that means something with it.

1 FEBRUARY 2004

Just come back from shopping for Madagascar with Mum. It was the last day of the sale at the climbing shop in Hull, so we went to get a few things on my kit-list. I now have some very scary-looking high-tech boots that will apparently keep my feet dry even if I go swimming. Then I have a bright purple sleeping bag that is shaped for a female body and will keep me warm in sub-zero temperatures. My sleeping mat can be folded down to microscopic scale. Mum and I just smiled and agreed with everything the shop assistant said. We had no idea what I should be buying or what anything did and so, as a result, I now have an all-singing all-dancing kit encased in a huge rucksack that I probably can't even carry. I'm surrounded by all this new shiny equipment and I haven't got a clue what any of it does. I'm terrified of this trip and yet it keeps on getting closer. Only five months away now.

The charity auction was held a few weeks ago; it was a huge success. We managed to raise close to £4,000 in the end, which will cover our visa costs and give us each an extra £300 or so to add to our own funds. It was the Madonna platinum disc that ended up raising the most money, with a signed cap from Jenson Button close behind. I came away with the pen signed by Tony Blair, one of the items I had contributed in the first place, and I had to pay £8 for the pleasure. The irony is I don't even want it. I was trying to raise the bidding and it turned out no one else was willing to pay more than £7 to take it home. Oh well, it might be worth something one day.

Went shopping with Emma and another friend Helen in the sales yesterday. I bought a T-shirt from French Connection along with some eyeliner (though I'm not entirely sure what I'm supposed to do with it) while Emma and Helen got some new jeans. Still don't have a job yet. Mum just keeps giving me money. I think she reckons if I'm out with my friends doing things then at least it gets me out of the house and stops me thinking about Dad. But however many times I go shopping, I don't think that's ever going to happen.

1 MARCH 2004

I'm in total teenage agony. Think I'm really getting to like a boy called Daniel. We've become really good friends, especially through the Youth Town Council meetings. (I was asked at school if I wanted to volunteer for this, and so I went along to meet new people and get some experience.) He's started coming round all the time, to talk, listen to music and watch films, but I think I want it to be more than that. He makes me laugh, is always really friendly and although he's not totally gorgeous I think he's quite cute. Mum doesn't know that he comes round as much as he does. I think she'd be upset if she found out I was lying to her, but I feel like I need to grow up and start experiencing new stuff – that includes finally getting a proper boyfriend. I'm scared he doesn't like me in the way that I like him, though. Think he wants to get back with his old girlfriend as well, which is so not helping the situation! I've invited him to my year eleven leavers' ball as my date and he's agreed to come –

but just as friends. Although, a couple of nights ago he came round to the house and was messing about dancing me round the room in preparation for the night!

Seems ridiculous to feel like this about him because we've known each other for ages and I've never fancied him before. It's weird. Maybe I just feel like this because I want someone there for me and he's the one boy that's always here and the only one that's actually shown any interest in me. The other three all have their boyfriends, and although I know Mum needs me and I need her, I also need someone to talk to who doesn't have the emotional attachment to all the shit we've been through that she does. I just want someone to love me for being me and to look after me. That probably sounds really selfish and horrible, especially when the one person Mum had to do all that is no longer here.

It doesn't really matter, though, because Daniel doesn't like me in that way. He was round here tonight with everyone else from BYTC, but he was totally flirting with other girls and although it was obviously pissing me off he didn't even notice. Think I'm going to have to accept the fact that I will be single and loveless for ever.

Oh my God. Just looked at the calendar next to my desk. It's 1 March. That means it's been over six months since Dad died and I haven't even noticed. I feel so disgusted with myself, guilty for letting him slip out of my thoughts. Since moving to Beverley it's been easier to live life without that day hanging over us. I feel torn between knowing I have to get on with stuff and feeling a sense of loyalty to Dad. I'm just terrified I'm going to forget him.

14 APRIL 2004

E aster seems to have arrived so quickly. School has become busier and busier, and I've had less time to think – probably a good thing. Life at school seems to be creeping back to normal. Abby and I have started talking again and I'm just grateful that we can be friends; I've learned there's not much point in keeping a grudge, not over something as trivial as a schoolgirl fallout. Despite the gap that grew between us, she has always been a good friend and I've missed her a lot. As long as she's here for me now, what does the past matter?

About a week or so before the Easter holidays we got a call at home from our family liaison police officer, the man I'd rather forget. A date for the inquest had been set – 15 April. Tomorrow. We were told where it was, at what time, and that we should let them know how many people would be attending. Mum said that she didn't want to go, that it would upset her too much. I was insistent that I wanted to be there. I have to know what is being said about him. Emma and Rachel weren't sure about it at first but then they both agreed that they would come. We telephoned back to let the officer know but then Mum got a call from the Coroner's Office, asking her to attend, as she would be required to take the stand and be questioned on the police statement she had given. She reluctantly agreed.

I'm exhausted. We've just come home from two weeks in Boston. Eleven days in a hotel room can be stressful at the best of times but when the four people in that room are dreading returning home you can start to get on each other's nerves. Emma had some really down days where she didn't want to come out with us or even get out of bed. I hate to admit it but her behaviour seemed to me to be getting more and more like Dad's, and it scared the hell out of me. Mum was, as always – just as she had been with Dad – a brilliant listener and patient every day. When Emma irritated me to the point of tears, Mum simply waited until she was ready to talk. The atmosphere on most days was stifling, however, and had it not been for us keeping up appearances for Kathryn's sake I doubt we all would have got through the holiday unscathed.

Kathryn showed us around campus, into the rooms where the intellectually brilliant sit and work on projects I could only ever hope to understand. I remember thinking how proud of her I was and how proud Dad would've been. He was meant to be with us on that holiday – just weeks before he died we sat looking on the internet for hotels to stay in, places to visit and things to do. I think it hurt Kathryn that he never got to see her there, to see what she had achieved. We walked round Harvard, where Kathryn was now having medical lectures. It all seemed so ironic. I remember that first visit and how I told Dad that I was going to go there. I didn't really know much about it then, had just heard about its reputation and how prestigious it was to get a place. On this second visit I discovered more, and I still want to go, but it doesn't seem as easy an accomplishment as it did when I was ten years old. It also doesn't seem likely, considering I still haven't been able to concentrate for long enough to start my GCSE revision. Mum keeps reminding me that if I want to make Dad proud I have to get good results. I, of course, keep making excuses, saying no one looks at your GCSE results when you start A-levels. But when she shouted at me on holiday I really wanted to put the blame on her. I wanted to say I couldn't revise when she was upset, that every time she cried it ruined my concentration, and that I was worried about her. But I knew, and still do know, that if I want to make things work and do well then it's up to me. I have to want to do it. The desire to succeed is there, but whether or not I can do the bit in between remains to be seen.

We found out when we were away that Kathryn has been having really bad nightmares about Dad. She says she drifts off to sleep quite happily but the situation that haunts her is always the same. It's a game show where she is the contestant. The host keeps firing questions at her, all of which she gets right, then the final question comes and the host tells her that if she gives the correct answer then her prize is that Dad will come back. Yet of course, she never knows the answer and wakes before the game can be completed. She's been seeing a grief counsellor about it and she might even have to have hypnosis so she can finish the dream and stop playing the game. It's horrible, yet I know it stems from her feelings of guilt; that she thinks she is somehow to blame for Dad no longer being here. Looking at her while we were away I saw in my sister someone who was physically and emotionally exhausted. She has always been a sort of idol to me – she's ridiculously intelligent, funny and charismatic, not to mention the fact that she was like a second mother to me. But the person I saw on holiday was not the one who looked out for her younger sisters but instead one who was much in need of love and attention herself. Her dark hair matched her equally dark eyes, making her skin look even paler in the Boston winter air. Leaving her was so painful because I knew all any of us wanted to do was stay and look after her, but we had to come home. After all, we have an inquest to attend.

We were due to fly home yesterday at 7.30 p.m., but we arrived at the airport to find the flight had been delayed until 8.30 p.m. So we sat in the departure lounge. Rachel and Emma read, and Mum and I people-watched. She often comments on passing people, normally quietly enough so only I can hear. She had been looking for several minutes at the people passing, the different cultures, dress senses and behaviours, and said she thought the human race was really strange. I wondered what people said about us when we passed. Did they make comments in the same way that Mum does? I asked her what she thought, and she replied that people could say what they wanted because she couldn't hear them. I said, 'Don't you care what people think?' She told me she cared what the people that mattered thought, but as for everyone else, their opinions were irrelevant, as long as she was happy with herself. I suppose she was right; she usually is about these kinds of things. After a six-hour overnight flight, then a two-hour journey through Heathrow airport, we met a 200-metre queue to get the thirty-minute shuttle drive to get our car, so we could drive the five and a half hours it would take for us to get home.

We arrived in Beverley, exhausted, at about 2.30 p.m, today. We emptied suitcases, picked up Missie from the kennels, opened the mountain of post stacked up behind the door – the usual stuff you do when you return from holiday. But then each of us retreated to our separate rooms and tried to find something suitable to wear for tomorrow.

I'm sitting here now, at the wooden desk in my bedroom, dressed in tomorrow's outfit. I chose similar clothes to the ones I wore to the funeral, mostly black with a pink flower pattern on my trousers. I'm worried about tomorrow. What will happen? What will they say? I've got no idea what it will be like. I guess I'll just have to wait and see. Going to bed now, though. I'm completely jet-lagged and very much looking forward to being lost in sleep.

15 APRIL 2004

Today's been very strange. Good in some ways, horrible in others. There's no other way to describe it than to start from the beginning and this morning when my alarm woke me up at about 7 a.m. About ten different alarms went off in the house at around the same time, so terrified were we that the time difference would cause us all to sleep in. I woke feeling like shit, and that feeling didn't get much better throughout the whole day.

Although the inquest wasn't due to start until 10 a.m., Mum decided we needed to leave the house at 8.30 a.m. for the twenty-minute drive into Hull. On the way, Rachel sent a text message to Auntie Liz, letting her know we were on our way, and got a text message back in reply: '*Am in Hull. See you guys there. Liz x*'. A couple of text messages later it emerged she'd arrived by train from Dundee last night and had stayed in the station hotel. We realised the inquest might be harder for her than we'd imagined. When you're so consumed by your own grief it's difficult to see past the cloudy screen of despair and watch how others deal with theirs.

Due to Mum's insistence that we left unnecessarily early, we arrived at the courtroom at 9 a.m. Luckily Marks & Spencer came to the rescue with their handy café just at the end of the street.

On the way there I passed a post boy who worked at the law firm where I went for my work experience last year. It was strange to think that the last time I was in a courtroom I was observing the lawyers, looking at my possible future. This time it would be from a totally different perspective.

That last time, my first time in court, I was attending a murder trial at the end of my work experience week. It was supposed to be a 'treat'. Chris, who was looking after me that day, had taken me to Hull Crown Court, shown me around, gave me a choice between triple rape and murder, and then left me sitting in courtroom number one. It was November, just over two months since Dad's death. As I sat in the public gallery I took no notice of the deceased's family sitting around me. I was shocked to discover I felt no empathy with them. I didn't notice whether or not the pathologist or toxicologist looked at them or not, or how they reacted to the witnesses giving evidence. I was hypnotised by the powerful people in wigs and the defendant behind the glass screen. But as the case was pieced together, it became far too real and painful for me to endure.

I'd chosen murder over triple rape, not knowing anything about the case, but it emerged that it was a woman who'd been killed. She'd been hit by a lorry. She was also suffering from depression and taking medication. It was on debate whether, as accused, her boyfriend, the driver of the vehicle, had killed her purposely or if she, after their violent argument, had flung herself under the wheels. During the description of the blood found on the side of the articulated vehicle I felt deeply sick. At the break I walked quickly outside, not stopping to undertake the customary bow to the judge. Returning to the office, Chris asked me if I wanted to go back after dinner. I declined, but didn't explain why.

After that day I had imagined what Dad's inquest would be like, and whether anyone would be blamed. The driver? Dad? I wasn't naive enough to think that there would be a trial. I knew enough about court processes to know there would be no judge and no jury, and that the coroner would be the one to make the final decision. But even after everything I had imagined, I was unprepared for the event.

Auntie Liz met us in the café. She walked in just as Emma rushed off to the toilet feeling physically ill. We were all feeling so nervous and restless. We left for Essex House at 9.35 a.m., still too early, but the waiting was irritating us all and we ran out of mindless things to say to each other.

Essex House is a large, ugly building opposite chambers in the Old Town. I was the only one who knew where it was, as I had met a friend there every day for lunch on my work experience. It's a building used for a variety of legal purposes – property dealings, commercial, litigation law, benefits claims, as well as inquests. I wondered afterwards how the men on reception knew as we walked through the door why we where there. Was it the morbid, nervous look on our faces? Our clothes? Or maybe it was the way Emma, Rachel, Mum and I walked through the doors clutching tissues and holding hands. One of the men simply said, 'Inquest?' and nodded us through to the door on the left. We followed the corridor round to a room full of chairs and a small group of people. To the left there was a small room, with a metal sign that read 'Courtroom: Silence'.

We were greeted by a woman in her early fifties. She had white-blonde hair and a string of pearls around her neck, like the hostess of a posh party, rather than a courtroom clerk. The five of us were quickly ushered through the empty courtroom and into a smaller room at the back. I noticed the bland décor, the tissues on the table, a pile of pens and a water cooler. I couldn't help thinking that if they'd put a punchbag in the corner it might make things seem a bit more realistic. To me that room was so false. It seemed to say: you're in here to avoid the witnesses, not because we feel sorry for you.

Our family liaison officer showed up again, sporting a new haircut more suitable for someone twenty years his junior. Seeing him again brought back painful memories of him clutching a mug of tea in our dining room at Elloughton. He told us that there were actually a large number of witnesses who would be taking the stand that day, including one man in particular who had to give evidence first, as he needed to leave. We were told this was unusual and that we shouldn't feel his evidence was significant just because he was first. I knew then that the evidence he was going to give would be bad. It was.

After we were told to take our seats in the courtroom (a basic room with red chairs and a few tables strewn about), Mr Nixon took the oath. He swore to tell the truth, the whole truth and nothing but the truth. Mr Nixon was an elderly man, a vet. Owned a silver 4×4, worked in Swanland. He was behind the lorry when it hit my dad, saw his body being thrown into the air and then land again on the grass verge. Mr Nixon had definitely seen my father, Mr Robert Griffin, lurch forward off the grass verge and into the path of the lorry.

I slumped in my seat. Mum began to cry. Emma and Rachel clutched each other's hands. Liz was seated at the end of the row, furthest from me, so I couldn't see her reaction. It was no doubt similar to ours.

Throughout his evidence Mr Nixon looked straight at the coroner, Mr Saul. Not once did he look straight ahead, as this would have meant making eye contact with me and watching the tears fall down my face as he gave his evidence.

Like the other witnesses still to come, Mr Nixon was asked three main questions: what was the weather like on 27 August 2003 and did this affect the visibility on the road? What were the driving conditions like on this day? And then the killer question, the one that crushed me every time: have you ever seen anybody running, walking or acting in a manner similar to Mr Griffin on this stretch of road before? Each witness's answer was virtually identical. The weather was fine so this meant that visibility and the driving conditions were excellent. And no, not one person had ever seen or heard of a pedestrian on the side of the A63.

After Mr Nixon came the pathologist. The courtroom was advised before proceedings began that if you were of a sensitive nature it might be advisable to wait outside during the pathologist's testimony, due to the nature of the evidence given. After Mr Nixon had finished nobody moved, but I wish I'd gone. Mr Saul asked the pathologist to describe the injuries sustained to the body as he had viewed it during the post-mortem.

The pathologist, whose name I cannot recall (I just remember he was a fairly elderly male), glanced briefly in our direction before beginning. He started by telling us the main damage was done to the chest cavity; ribs 1, 2, 3 and 4 on both sides were broken, the clavicle was broken, the sternum fractured, both shoulder bones damaged and there was a collapsed lung. He also had massive head injuries and facial fractures on the right side of his body. The cause of death was apparently 'multiple injuries', a clouded term for the fact that there were so many things wrong that he didn't have a cat in hell's chance of survival. When asked if Mr Griffin's death would have been instantaneous the pathologist replied, 'Yes, most definitely.'

Mr Saul repeated the question several times, only to receive the same answer. He then looked over to us and said that he could affirm that death had been instant and at least no pain had been endured by the deceased. He then looked down at his papers, ready to call the next witness. I wondered if saying what he had just said was for our benefit, trying to make us feel better, or whether he had said it for himself.

Listening to the pathologist's evidence took me back to my bedroom at Elloughton and the dark nights when I lay in bed, imagining the incident. Sitting in that courtroom, I tried to imagine what 'instant death' would feel like. Over in a matter of seconds. I envisaged it in slow motion: the first foot leaves the grass verge, the lorry just metres away, the second foot comes around in front as the body is turned away from the traffic, towards the footbridge, towards home. As the body turns slightly and the right side makes impact with the lorry's cab, smashing the indicator and headlight, trapping red fibres from his running T-shirt in the broken glass, is eye contact made with the driver? Is he crying? Does he feel pain as his bones are broken or does it all just go black, emptiness as his brain switches off? What was his last thought? Did he go unconscious for a few seconds before death? In those few seconds of impact, what did he feel? Fear? Hope? Regret over what he may have done? Who knows?

Mr Saul called for his next witness, or victim. It was Mum. I squeezed her hand and Emma looked at her, pleadingly almost, as she rose. She too was asked to take the oath. With the Bible in her right hand, she, like Mr Nixon, swore to tell the truth, the whole truth and nothing but the truth. As she sat next to Mr Saul, facing the courtroom, she selected a new tissue from the box in front of her. She confirmed her name, her birth date and her address at the time of my father's death.

The coroner asked her how long she had been married to my dad and to confirm how long he'd had depression. She choked back her tears when she told the court they'd been married for twenty-five years; it had been their silver wedding anniversary just over a month before the accident. For the remainder of the questions she answered with a nod or just a one-word answer, and by the end of her questioning she had given up trying to hide the tears than ran down her face. Just before she stepped down from the stand Mr Saul asked her if there was anything more she wanted to say. She faced the court and decided that yes, there was. Mum glanced across at us before she spoke, and I got the feeling that although it would be Mr Saul deciding the outcome, she was directing her opinion not at him but at the row of witnesses at the other side of the room, as if they were the ones that needed convincing.

She said that if Dad had really wanted to end it he would not have done it that way; that there were other ways that wouldn't have put so many people's lives at risk.

The inquest progressed. Each witness was called up by their surname and title, and we were given a little introduction as to what they did for a living and the reason they were travelling on the A63 that morning. Of all the witnesses only one looked directly at us, 'the bereaved', as he walked towards the stand. He was some kind of goods driver working in Hull and the surrounding vicinity. I could tell he was trying to be as nice as possible as he gave his evidence and, as he was doing so, I realised why he could afford to be so nice: he really had not seen anything of any significance. He was behind the truck, in his car, and all he saw was a body being tossed up into the air, like a rag doll or a dummy, in his words. He hadn't seen Dad before or after this moment and didn't see the impact, therefore he had nothing condemning to say and, from our point of view, his evidence was pointless.

Throughout the inquest I had been studying the faces of the witnesses around me, trying to work out who the driver of the lorry might be. All I knew about him before the inquest was that he was in his mid-thirties and came from Sussex. There were about twelve men in the room and by the break in the proceedings I had eliminated the police officers, Mr Nixon, two more male witnesses who had already spoken and any male who was obviously over fifty. This left me with three men. Eventually there was only one left. When he got up to speak it was obvious who he was. He was fairly tall and slim with short blond hair. He had been sitting in the row behind us for the entire proceedings, his partner by his side.

He didn't say anything I didn't already know. In his view he had seen Dad lurch forward into the path of the truck. He was not at full height and therefore there was a possibility he could have stumbled, but the driver did not see. I was hardly listening to what the guy was saying, just staring intently at his face; every so often he would look over at us but he could not hold my gaze for more than a few seconds. At the end of his evidence he gave his sincerest condolences to the family. I felt sorry for him. I really did. He will have to live with what happened for the rest of his life. Yet at the same time as I felt pity I was still so angry. As stupid as it was, there was part of me that believed on that day the driver could have done something to prevent Dad dying, although I knew deep down nothing could have.

We had a short break while the coroner stepped outside to make his decision. Other people chatted but we just held hands and waited in silence. When he returned he took his place once more at the front of the room. Everyone was quiet and he began to speak. After a minute or so, I breathed a small sigh of relief because I felt pretty sure of the way it was going to go.

He started by saying that to give a verdict of suicide he had to be 100 per cent sure that the person in question had definitely intended to take his own life and that there were no other possibilities. He then went on to say that although there were many witnesses who seemed to suggest Mr Griffin had intentionally thrown himself in front of the lorry, he had also left a note to say he would be returning home, he had a key around his neck and other witnesses had testified to say there was a definite possibility that Mr Griffin had tripped or fallen into the lorry's path. In Mr Saul's words: 'There is no way that I can say Mr Griffin intentionally took his own life on that day because I have serious doubt. Therefore I must record an open verdict in this case.'

We were just relieved, not even at the verdict as such because I think deep down we knew there was only a slim possibility it could actually be called suicide. We were just relieved for it to be eventually over.

It was over in the courtroom at least. Before we left, Mum ran off in search of the driver. She wanted to apologise, to say sorry for Dad or Fate choosing his vehicle over someone else's. We were about to leave when the clerk came over. She mentioned that there had been two people sitting in the courtroom whom, we might have noticed, didn't give evidence. These two were journalists, one from the *Hull Daily Mail*, our local paper, and the other from the *Yorkshire Post*, the acclaimed regional paper. The clerk asked if we would like to talk to them. I was hesitant at first. The last thing I wanted was for our business to become local gossip, and I knew that that would have been the last thing Dad would have wanted either.

We decided that because the journalists had sat through the entire inquest they would make their own mind up about the evidence given and, so far as we were concerned, we would have nothing to lose by giving our side of the story.

We were shown into a smaller room just outside the courtroom. The male and female journalists shared the sofa and we gathered on the chairs surrounding it. The lady with the pearls also joined us, apparently as a 'court representative', but I couldn't help thinking that deep down she was just nosy.

At first they were gentle with us. They began by asking our names and ages and offering us their sincerest condolences. They were particularly sympathetic towards Mum, who was still shedding tears. Then the questions came thick and fast. Were we happy with the result of the inquest? Did we think it was suicide? How long had Dad been ill for? Was it difficult to live with? The questions kept coming and they kept jotting things down on their little pads. I didn't know what to say or how to respond to their questions. I was frightened of mentioning the wrong thing and scared that Mum was being too trusting. They kept asking her if he'd ever shown suicidal signs before or if he really was unhappy in his life. She was emotional and confided in them how hard it had been to live with sometimes when he was very 'black', as if he physically changed colour when he was down. Emma and Rachel and I tried to put in our opinion, to tell them what an amazing father he'd been, yet I could tell they weren't really listening. When we spoke their pens hardly touched paper. After about five minutes in the small room, and after Mum had been reduced to tears once more, the journalists decided they had finished and got up to leave. We were told both newspapers would be publishing the story tomorrow.

Following the inquest, we went out for lunch and rang Kathryn in America. She was pleased that the result had been an open verdict but when we told her that the journalists had been asking questions she sounded worried. I hope she doesn't have a reason to be. It seems so ridiculous that after years of keeping his secret protected so successfully Dad should lose his privacy through the words of two local journalists simply out to find a good story.

20 APRIL 2004

Since the inquest Mum's been in a bit of a mess. The two days following it she spent in bed, the whole shock of his death hitting her all over again. She says it seems as though a big door has been closed and yet she's not ready to move on. I guess that hearing the coroner's decision is some kind of a milestone in this little part of my life. Now that it has happened and been dealt with, we are supposed to carry on to the next stage. I decided on the night of the inquest what I needed to do in order to move on. I sat by the phone for about half an hour before I plucked up the courage to do it.

Up to that point in my life I had told no one about my family's secret. So far as any of my friends knew, Dad's death last August had been a plain and simple accident and there was nothing more to it. I thought that their view might be totally different after the story of the inquest appeared in the papers. Deep down I didn't care what most people thought when they saw the story; what mattered to me were my friends' opinions. I was terrified that if my close friends saw it they would be upset that I hadn't confided in them about my problems.

Hands shaking, I rang my best friend Emma first. She was her usual chirpy self when she answered. My voice was wobbly as I told her I had something I wanted her to know. I started by telling her that the reason I'd been busy the other morning was because I'd been to the inquest. I then told her the reason there'd been an inquest and what was brought up. I slowly explained about Dad's depression and the implications it had on the inquest and what some people could be suggesting had happened.

When I'd finished she just said, 'Well, you know I'm always here if you want a chat. I'm sure the papers will be fine but if anyone says anything I'll have a word.' That was it. No questions, no shock, no disappointment in me for keeping it from her. She simply understood. Dad's illness had no effect on her view of me.

I was so relieved. I replaced the handset then searched through my mobile phone for Daniel's house number. I've long since realised that we're never going to be more than just friends but a brilliant friend he has been, especially recently, and he is always there to talk about family stuff. (Plus, I still have the year eleven ball to look forward to!) His reaction was pretty much the same as Emma's, although he wanted to come round and give me a big hug.

It sounds awful to say I was truly amazed at their reactions. Perhaps I should have had a little more faith in my own friends, but maybe it's fair to say I base my judgement of them on other people's reactions in the past. When Dad was younger he'd experienced a bad reception when his work colleagues realised something wasn't quite right and as a result he was 'asked to leave' two of his jobs. Maybe it would have been different if he'd been in a different job but it seems that when a man is handling someone else's money it's important that his mental health is nothing less than perfect. Sounds perfectly normal, doesn't it? Just like we might not want someone with mental health issues treating us in our hospitals or teaching our kids in our schools. But considering that just over one in four people in Britain are said to suffer from mental health problems at one time, we're pretty screwed. In fact, 9.2 per cent of the population apparently suffers from mild depression or anxiety, so are those people considered OK? They are still classed as mentally unstable. Just where do we draw the line? An item on the news not long ago said that, according to the World Health Organisation, depression will be the second most common killer in the world by 2020, surpassing both heart disease and AIDS. Then where will we be?

The journalists in the courtroom both produced pieces that contrasted greatly with the praise and sympathy expressed in the press in the week following the accident. The article in the *Hull Daily Mail*, our local paper, stated in its headline that Dad had 'acted strangely' before being 'killed by truck' and opened with the phrase: 'A father of four was killed instantly when he "lurched" in front of an articulated truck on a dual carriageway.' Right at the very end, in the very last sentence, in the corner of the article, the journalist mentioned the open verdict that was recorded. Scan the article and you'll easily miss it.

The second article talked of his long-running depression as if his illness had completely encompassed him.

Yesterday I went for a walk with Helen, one of my school friends. I talked to her about my family a bit and explained that the newspaper articles had really upset me.

'Oh, yeah,' she said. 'It must have done because loads of people were going round saying really stupid stuff about what actually happened.'

'Stupid stuff? Like what? Who?' I became concerned. I'd been naive enough to think that either no one had seen the stories, or that they cared enough not to allow it to become school corridor gossip.

'Well, one person started telling people that your dad had jumped off the footbridge near your house directly into the lorry's path.' The girl she mentioned I'd thought was a friend of mine. The suggestion seemed ridiculous at the time. After all, I knew that the place he was actually killed was at least a hundred feet from the bridge; it would had to have been a bloody good jump!

'That's stupid,' I retorted. 'Why the hell would she say something like that? The papers didn't even say that it was suicide. It was an open verdict!'

'It was? Oh. I thought they had said that it was definitely suicide.'

And there it was. The proof that, regardless of the truth, people will think what the hell they want to, as long as it makes a good story.

Yet after my initial anger I began to think that maybe the truth didn't matter anyway. After all, I didn't even know the real truth; all I knew was that an open verdict meant uncertainty, his choice or Fate. My truth, my reality that I had to face was that, regardless of what he may or may not have done, he loved me and my family, and that if he did kill himself he did it for us and no one else. But hell, who knows what was going through his mind that day? If other people want to create some kind of fantasy around the story then let them. Truth is simply a nice idea, a reality we try to create for ourselves for our own peace of mind. Yet whether I like it or not, the truth is out and people now know something of what my family was really like behind our perfect façade.

20 MAY 2004

Yesterday was my last day of school. Leaving in my uniform for the last time felt amazing. Total freedom! An afternoon of celebrations was followed by the year eleven ball last night. It was held at a pub in a town nearby. I wore the dress that I had bought from Macy's in Boston last month. It's long black silk with thin spaghetti straps and the front panel is covered in white embroidered flowers. At the back there's a white silk panel with black criss-cross detail. It's so pretty. All the girls had their hair done in town after school and then I came home to get ready at mine. Daniel came round just before we were about to leave. He looked really smart in his suit but I definitely think we should stay friends now; I just don't like him in that way any more. He did bring me a rose, though, which made me feel very special. Lucy came round with her date, Tom, and we were all taken to the hotel.

I was nervous before we went and so saw an opportunity to get properly drunk. I've never really been that much into drinking, but my friends have all been going out drinking more and more often. When I do drink I realise it gives me a confidence I don't usually have, so in awkward situations it normally helps. I downed most of the champagne that we'd opened at the house and when we arrived at the Jarvis I was pretty drunk. I tripped over my dress on the stairs and fell pretty much flat on my face. I'm sure I was embarrassed at the time but didn't even remember doing it until this morning. How awful is that?

We got there and I spotted that my friend Maddy had come with a friend of hers in the year above, Mark. I knew of him because he lives near a few of my friends and sometimes goes to the park with them but I'd never really spoken to him before. He is gorgeous, though. He's nearly 6 ft with short, spiky brown hair, blue eyes and, most importantly, a beautiful smile. All thoughts about being with anyone else were totally thrown out the window. I couldn't believe it when he started talking to me and even bought me a drink (not that I needed it the state I was in). We chatted quite a few times during the night but then everyone started dancing to the sounds of the *Grease* mega-mix and *Saturday Night Fever* and I lost sight of him. Next time I saw him he was on the dance floor with Ruth, a very pretty but fairly dull girl in my year. He looked at me and then leaned in to kiss her. I was heartbroken but because I was full to the brim with champagne it just made me determined to find someone else and I ashamedly went and 'pulled' my friend Jess's date. I'm so ashamed to think of it now because I didn't even like him that much. Feeling very rough now and very sorry for myself, especially now that a month of revision looms in front of me. Can't believe my exams have come around this quickly. I feel so unprepared.

12 JUNE 2004

Argh, I'm so excited! Mark came round last night! It was so random how it happened. I was just on the internet chatting to some friends on MSN messenger when he came online and started talking to me. We both mentioned that we were bored at home and how sad it was that we were stuck in on a Friday night. I had the house to myself as Mum was going out with the girls and so I took the plunge and asked him if he wanted to come round. I couldn't believe it when he said yes! He turned up at my door looking really hot in a yellow T-shirt and jeans. Mum saw him before she went out and even said he was good-looking!

We got a film out, then ordered a pizza and just chatted in the lounge. I really, really fancied him, though, and wanted it to be less like friends, so, with a little help from Mum's alcohol store, I had a few drinks to help me stop being so nervous around him and eventually asked if he wanted to go upstairs to listen to some music. I couldn't tell whether or not he liked me as I liked him but I decided just to go for it and see what happened. He was sitting on my bed when I just kissed him. God, I was so relieved when he kissed me back. He left pretty much soon after that but I was so happy, jumping around the house like a jack-in-a-box! I just hope this time it works and something actually comes from it, rather than just being an empty kiss like the rest.

Have got the last of my injections for Madagascar tomorrow. Yellow fever and the final hepatitis A and hepatitis B booster vaccinations. After the auction I raised the rest of the money for the trip by doing more bag packing at supermarkets and running my sweet stall in school at lunchtime. We also received small donations from local companies. Next week I have to start taking a course of malaria tablets, though they have warned me that suicidal thoughts can be a side effect. Whoopee. As if it wasn't likely enough already.

30 JUNE 2004

Yesterday was the last day of exams and today is the day before I go to Madagascar, so last night we had a bit of a party at Emma's house, jointly in celebration for the beginning of summer and to say goodbye to me. I was so excited all afternoon because I'd been texting Mark and he said he would come round, but I was nervous because I really wanted something to happen. The party started at 7 p.m. We put up gazebos in the back garden, started a BBQ and had bought loads of alcohol and food. About forty or so people turned up, a lot of my friends brought me good luck cards and my friend Rob arrived with a notebook that he'd made people sign to say good luck before I left. I felt as though I was going away for a year, not just a month! Abby and Helen gave me a teddy bear to take with me so I wouldn't be so lonely in my amazing super-shiny sleeping bag. It's extra weight to carry but worth it, if only to remind me I have real friends at home.

Mark was late and I was getting worried that he wouldn't come. He eventually arrived, though, accompanied by two girls from his year, which surprised me a bit. We've been getting really close recently and I thought it was fairly obvious that something was going to happen last night. I talked to a few people then went over to chat to him, but he was really cold and distant. I thought at first that it might have been me just misreading the signals. Towards the end of the night I thought I'd try again so I went over to chat, and things were going really well until I leaned in to kiss him. Straight away he pushed me backwards and told me he didn't want anything to happen between us. I was really shocked and completely taken aback. I couldn't (and still can't) understand why he was being so horrible. I ran off and, though I'm ashamed to say it now, cried to Emma in her kitchen. He made me really angry as well as upset, because the rejection had made me feel completely worthless; if he didn't want me, I reasoned, then nobody would.

I felt so ugly and horrible, and needed to up my confidence again, so stupidly I drank a bottle of wine, downed plenty of shots and kissed three other boys in front of him. I'm sure it didn't make the prospect of being with me any more appealing to him but it definitely made me feel better about myself at the time. It was almost as if I was trying to prove to him that someone did find me attractive.

This morning, though, like every morning after I've made a drunken fool out of myself, I just feel ashamed and embarrassed and very much looking forward to leaving the country tomorrow.

I'm hoping Madagascar will give me the opportunity to look at myself and really ask what the fuck I am doing. The minute I have a problem or Mum's upset, I respond by going out with my friends, getting absolutely hammered and spending the night searching for someone who makes me feel loved. I had my first visit to a club in Hull a couple of weeks ago, and because I was so nervous about getting in and not appearing underage, I went a bit overboard with drinking and pulled some random 21-year-old. I've got to realise that the problems I have accepting myself are not gonna be solved by a groping session with some random guy when I'm completely out of it. I know that, in the future, going out and drinking in town will become the norm, and I have to learn how to handle myself.

I just hope this trip is going to be everything I expect of it. My huge green rucksack is fully packed with all my new essentials: penknife, cutlery, sleeping bag and basic clothing (though I'm not looking forward to the fact that I can only take three pairs of underwear with me). I'm terrified about spending a whole month with people I don't know, but I'm excited, too, and although it sounds awful to say it I'm looking forward to getting away from home and spending some time away from Mum. I love her to bits, I really do, but since Dad died we've spent all our time together and I've come to realise that when she's upset there's nothing I can do to make it better. The love I can give her is just not enough, it cannot mend the hole. I think

I just need some time off from trying to fight a losing battle.

Not taking my diary with me so will write in a month. Here's hoping I come back unscathed!

31 JULY 2004

Got back from Madagascar this morning. It was the single most amazing experience I've ever had in my life and I've got my diary out straight away in the need to write it all down before it leaks from my memory and I sink back into my normal routine.

I was really scared before I went, mainly because I didn't know any of the people I was going with and because I presumed most of them were posh little rich girls. Our group, from the outside, looked about as privileged as possible. The eight girls came from my mum's private school, and I thought I might become irritated by their assumed airs and graces. Yet, after a closer look at our group, I was proved very wrong.

One girl a year older than myself had lost her sister in a riding accident just a week before Dad died. Another member had a brother in intensive care after serious health issues. Our female leader suffered from rheumatoid arthritis despite only being in her early thirties. Yet despite all our grievances as a group, I felt we were pretty much silenced as our flight touched down in Antananarivo (the capital city).

I had never visited a developing country before. My only brush with poverty had been our two holidays in the Caribbean when we had passed through shanty towns. I had never really given a second thought to what life would be like for people living in poor conditions. Yet arriving at the Hotel Raphia, around a £1 a night for a room and shared bathroom in peak season, I began to have many thoughts. I looked around from the hotel roof and saw makeshift housing, beggars in the street, filth and grime. I couldn't comprehend that this place was a capital city. I had seen the homeless hiding out in the doorways of London's stores many times before but here there were thousands of buildings lining the pavements, all of them home to the most unfortunate people I'd ever seen.

I only really realised the extent of the problem when we arrived at Akany Avoko, a refuge centre for (predominantly) teenage girls who had either got into trouble for petty crime or had been orphaned. Akany Avoko had started out as an overspill for the juvenile courts, a place for youngsters to go when all other possibilities had been exhausted or simply when no one else wanted them. Now it was a place for the destitute and the unloved. Approximately ninety girls and fifteen boys lived at this shelter just outside the city; the majority of them had no relatives, no belongings and no prospects, and all their hope now rested on Steve, the English volunteer who ran the shelter, and his Malagasy wife.

A girl ran up to me and threw her arms around my waist as we arrived. A good seven inches below my 5ft 2in, I presumed she was about ten or eleven years old. I later found out she was eighteen and that her poor height was due to severe malnutrition in childhood. She also spoke very little, tormented from years of abuse at the hands of her poverty-stricken parents. She stood and hugged me for two hours. I remember being shocked at the sheer number of children all standing around staring at us. To them we had everything they wanted, everything they longed for. Halfway through our evening meal (rice and vegetables) an eight-year-old girl arrived, having been found wandering the city. She said nothing, but the look on her face was pure misery. We learned from her finder that in the past few days, both her parents had died and she had several younger brothers and sisters, all now scattered across the country. As the tears slowly fell from her eyes, a large hole of emptiness appeared in my stomach, yet I felt like the luckiest person in the world. I realised just how much I had and, however much I lost, emotionally or in material terms, I would never be as bare and empty as those children at Akany Avoko.

Over the following days I met more unfortunate kids, heard stories that both horrified me and filled me with hope. In the girls' dormitories the walls were covered in posters from ancient American magazines; strong, rich, beautiful Western women stared back at me. Jennifer Aniston, Britney Spears and Jennifer Lopez were these teenagers' heroines. All they wanted was a chance in life. Over the week I spent there I thought of all the opportunities I had passed up in life, all the things I can never be bothered to do, all the moments I'd wasted. A fourteen-year-old called Tina told me she wanted to be a pop star; she had a beautiful voice. She gazed longingly at adverts for the Malagasy version of *Pop Idol*, knowing she would never get that chance. In such a short time I reviewed everything I'd ever done, regretted the majority of things that I hadn't done and vowed to do so much more. Everything that had ever happened to me was put into the 'bigger picture'. I was given just what I needed: perspective.

The whole trip was such a culture shock. While we were trekking up hills and taking in our stunning environment, the sticky hands of small children would be tugging at our walking trousers in the hope of a square of chocolate or a biscuit we had brought along for an energy snack. We performed heads, shoulders, knees and toes to a group of local villagers on a hillside surrounding a beautiful lake. Their faces lit up as they tried to teach it back to us in Malagasy. It was the look on people's faces that really struck me, a look of pure gratitude, as though we were the kindest people they had ever met. They appreciated the tiny little things that we, in our lavish lives, forget. In one hotel I left a pair of my old trainers in a dustbin, to save me carrying the extra weight any further. About an hour later when loading up the minibus (or *taxi-bousse* as it's called over there) I saw a cleaner holding up my smelly shoes to her friend in amazement. A small crowd had gathered around her and my trainers, all of them marvelling at her find. It just made me giggle, grateful that I could do something good, however small.

It was a trip that made me realise things about myself, too. The biggest trek we did was a climb up to the summit of Pic Boby, at 2,658 m Madagascar's highest accessible mountain. It's not a hard climb for an experienced climber but the fact that we weren't the fittest of groups meant that our team leader didn't have much hope in us all reaching the peak. He listed the girls that he thought would make it, about four out of the nine of us, me not included. That just made me more determined than ever to complete it. It was a long day. We left two girls at the bottom, those who were feeling too ill even to contemplate the climb. Halfway up another girl and our female leader turned back. The rest of us (after a very scary shuffle over a patch of ice at the top) made it to the summit. I was so proud of myself to know that I'd achieved something really positive, all by myself. The night before I'd told Jim, our team leader, all about Dad. Standing there on the top of Pic Boby, sheltering from the powerful wind and thick fog, he leaned over and whispered in my ear, 'Your dad would be proud.'

Back at home now I feel full of hope and the prospect of change. I honestly believe this trip has changed me, hopefully for the better, and soon I'll be able to look forward and not back. Looking forward is definitely on my mind right now, as I get my GCSE results in less than a month. I'm totally terrified!

Mum is still feeling pretty low and finding it hard to forget. Although forget is the wrong word. The problem is that she's remembering the wrong things; she's looking back to last August and the pain that came with Dad's death rather than the good memories that came coupled with his life.

Emma and Kathryn are both home from uni at the minute and that is making things a bit easier. It fills up her days and avoids the silence. We're also going on holiday in August, to Sorrento in Italy. I can't wait.

15 AUGUST 2004

I t's a gorgeous day today. I'm lying on my huge sleigh bed, having just tidied my room. Strange how when things are in their right place it gives you the feeling that everything else in your life is calm and ordered. It was getting pretty disgusting and when you couldn't really see my carpet any more Mum decided it had gone too far and yelled at me to sort it out. Not really been up to much for the last couple of days because of course it's still the summer holidays and I've still got nearly two weeks until GCSE results. I've just been spending days with Mum, going shopping or visiting friends. I still haven't got myself a job because I just haven't seemed to find the motivation, and there's always an excuse not to. Have been going out with my friends still, just into town and to a nightclub, pretty similar to how life was before I went away. It's such a strange club, though. We go because they'll let anyone in and as long as you can rattle off a birth date that makes you over eighteen there's no problem. But the regulars there are – how can I say this? . . . alternative.

The majority of the bar staff have dyed black hair and these things in their ears called flesh tunnels. You get your ear pierced and then stretch the piercing to put in a tiny black tunnel. As the piercing heals you put in larger and larger tunnels until the ear lobe is completely stretched and you have a huge hole through it. The only thing to really distinguish the staff is how long they'd had their flesh tunnels for and so how close to their shoulders their ear lobes hang. The club itself is painted completely black inside, with small seating areas. There are rooms connected by narrow corridors and doorways. In the front room the regular people hang out; they range from fifteen to about fifty (I'm not joking). The outfits are anything from jeans and a T-shirt to full bondage gear. It's pretty scary. Downstairs they play rock and heavy metal music – basically anything people can scream along or jump up and down to. Upstairs it's like a completely different place. You go up a narrow spiral staircase (which I'm sure is a major fire hazard) and then it opens up into two tiny rooms with low ceilings. It's much brighter up there, though I'm not sure if that's more to do with the absence of black clothing than the actual lighting. The brighter atmosphere is probably to do with the music, too; they play 1960s and 1970s classics mixed with Motown. Every time we go, Emma and I request either 'Don't Stop Me Now' by Queen or 'Play That Funky Music' by Wild Cherry.

Upstairs there are mainly students, just there for the cheap alcohol, good music and naive underage girls like me and my friends, who have normally drunk way too much. Other regulars include those called 'emo', apparently it stands for a style of music called 'emotional hardcore' or 'emocore'. The fashion style is all about being individual and not following trends but I don't get it. It's a style in itself and they all end up just looking the same. Apparently it's about being in touch with your sensitive side, writing poems about the darkness of the world and being melancholy or 'emotional'. I just don't get it. We create all these little groups so we can be original or express ourselves or some such crap, but isn't it just another way of feeling like you belong? Soon it will be the normal person, the regular jeans and T-shirt wearing teenager who becomes original because a top that's not customised or a pair of trousers that aren't covered in badges and stickers will be unusual.

Apparently emos are different from goths, and from skaters, and then chav culture is a whole different ball game. Someone told me recently chav has just been put in the dictionary. I don't think most teenagers even know what it means so how are the old folks at the Oxford Dictionary place supposed to know? I thought chavs were like the kids that like to hang around in bus stops and drink cider in the local park, but apparently it's more about an obsession with designer labels, gold jewellery, and dance and R&B music. I like dance. I like designer clothes. But I want to be original and I like some 'emo' music. So where do I fit in? Maybe if I change to fit one of these stereotypes I'll feel better. I think that's one of the reasons I get really drunk every time I go out; it seems to be the only thing all these groups have in common and the only way I can fit in and feel comfortable.

It's like the other day. I went into Hull with Jess, Emma and Helen. We were in Boots looking at the make-up and I decided I was going to buy some for going out that night. There were all these different brands in front of me – a confusion of offers and prices, and rows and rows of endless products. I started out with the eyeshadows, over a hundred different colours. Which did I want? I had no idea. If I bought one, would it make me a better person than another one? Apparently anything too bright or white was too chavvy while anything too outlandish or dark was either emo or too gothic. So I was left with a range of colours that were considered socially OK. I was so confused. I was terrified of picking one up and it being the wrong colour. It's so ridiculous, it makes me feel that I have no identity. Just because you don't wholly fit into one group or another it's as if you're a social outcast. Arrghh! It drives me crazy. Surely I'm not the only one that just doesn't get it? Sometimes I wish someone would come along and stick a label on me. At least then I could get on with moulding into that specification. At the minute I feel as if I'm playing that child's game where you have to drop the right-shaped blocks into the right-shaped hole. Except I'm the shape that the child keeps bashing against the hole because it won't go through. I just don't fit! Maybe all us odd shapes can get together one day and form an anti-group group, one where we all belong.

26 AUGUST 2004

Got my GCSE results this morning. The phone went at 8 o'clock. It was Mrs Vincent, the headteacher, asking me to go in early to open my results live on Radio Humberside. I went in, not knowing whether this would mean I'd done well or very badly. I knew I hadn't done anywhere near enough work. I'd been too preoccupied with myself and my messy thoughts to even think about school last year. Standing there in the office, palms sweating, legs shaking, I had a thought. I asked myself if, deep down, it mattered to me how I'd done. I knew that my study leave had lacked any real revision and that maybe I would be disappointed with myself if I got bad results, yet this wasn't what I was worried about. I was scared Mum would feel let down, anxious the girl standing next to me would have got better results, worried that people would laugh if I'd done badly. Deep down I was scared about what *everyone else* would say. Dad once said that if you ignored everything around you – the people, the material things we convince ourselves we need – if you can block everything else out and just concentrate on yourself and what's inside you, and then search for your own happiness, that self-satisfaction that should exist somewhere in your soul. Unless you find that self-happiness, that belief that deep down you're OK, well, basically you're a bit screwed. Suddenly I realised that this was about me and no one else.

I stared at the results on the page and a stir in my stomach told me I was satisfied. The girl next to me did get better results, but I knew that in a matter of weeks people would stop asking, so I already didn't care. Mum said she was happy as long as I'd tried my best. So really, I was my biggest critic, the one that had to be impressed, and that, I realised, was the way it was always going to be. Other people change, move in and out of your life, your environment, and life's scenery is constantly altering, yet the one thing you always have to live with is yourself. The little voices criticising you will always be there so you have to learn to accept them. The battle with your inner demons is a daily one that we all have to deal with, on one scale or another. On occasion, some people, like Dad, just believe they're never going to win.

We're leaving for Italy at two o'clock this afternoon, just Mum, Kathryn, Emma and me. Rachel is in America, working for a Jewish holiday camp. I'm really looking forward to it; a week away to prepare for the next big stage in my life, sixth form.

Tomorrow will be the one year anniversary. I know that these milestones do not really matter. What difference does it make if one extra day makes up a whole year of hell or only 364 days? What matters is that gradually, I believe, we're making progress as a family. We're moving on – slowly, yes, but moving none-the-less. Like an old train moving out of a station, it takes time to build up the strength, but we're definitely gathering speed and soon we'll be well on our way.

20 SEPTEMBER 2004

Today would have been Dad's forty-ninth birthday, yet, as I quietly remember him, I'm no longer sitting here crying over the pain of him not being here. Instead I hope he's just watching (and probably laughing at) me as I struggle over life's little hurdles.

For me September has always meant the start of a new school year. Sharpening new pencils, naming new clothes, anticipating the year ahead. A new start and a new experience. This September has been no different. I was excited at the prospect of starting sixth form, starting new subjects and, most importantly, making new friends and meeting new people.

The first two weeks have been great. I've settled into my subjects. English Literature has provided me with a new outlet for random discussion, usually about something deep and meaningful like happiness and life experiences, but I occasionally feel the discussion can get a little too close for comfort. Upon discussing

William Blake's *Songs of Innocence and Experience*, we talked about what made you lose innocence or change your outlook on life. I spoke about there being a time or a situation when you realise it's not all going to work out as you want it to. My teacher asked, mockingly, what had happened to me in my short life to give me that view. The class turned round to face me, and I began to shake, my palms sweating. I stared intently at him, silently pleading him not to probe further. I was still so scared about how people would view me, my fears about prejudice now set in stone. In the end I said that when you lose someone close to you, you also lose faith and optimism about the world around you. There was another person in the class who had also lost a parent at a young age, and I could tell that he too had been upset by the teacher's comments.

This week, however, everything seems to have altered, and it's like being back in school last year when the newspaper articles came out and I felt everyone was whispering about me behind my back. I guess in a year group of 140 sixteen- and seventeen-year-olds, bitchiness is hard to avoid. Some have started to analyse people's clothes, music choice, flirting and even the charities they support. A few lads in my year have begun to call me and my friends 'fake'. Other people call us 'the cheerleaders'. I just like to organise charity events and raise money for causes I believe in. What do they want me to do? Reveal to everyone all the emotions that run through my head on a daily basis?

I want to challenge them to find me someone who

doesn't put on an act at least sometimes, someone who acts the same in every single situation. That person does not exist. My way of putting on a mask in front of different people is a defence mechanism to protect me from everyday knocks. If I wore on my sleeve the sorrow I feel for everything that has happened to me or everything I have witnessed, I would be emotionally exhausted, constantly telling everyone my life story. Yet the side of me that involves Dad is just one angle of my personality. No person is one-dimensional. The office boss is not the same strict slave-driver at home as he is at work. A rape victim's vulnerability is only occasionally revealed to a partner, family member or counsellor. A one-dimensional unmasked person could exist only in the form of a newborn child, someone free of all experience and painfully open to life's lessons.

Surely before we can judge someone, before we can analyse or discriminate, we must first investigate thoroughly. If you bite into the shiny, appetising surface of an apple and then it turns out to be rotten on the other side, is it not your fault for not looking carefully enough at it rather than the apple's fault for being deceptive? Mum's main fear about Dad's illness was that if people found out about it they would judge him before knowing the facts, before realising his depression was an irrelevance, just a different angle to his multi-dimensional personality. Maybe we're all guilty of pulling down a mask once in a while. I think it's part of human nature to hide the bits of yourself you think others won't find appealing, and a lot of people forget that. People with mental health problems are human at the end of the day, just wired a little differently.

There are some benefits to life in sixth form, though. I've just started talking to Mark again and found that my old feelings for him are still there, though I'm scared he still doesn't want me. But there are always plenty of other guys and I'm sure one of them must be able to put up with me! Went out at the weekend with my friends. I got really drunk (as usual) and met a guy called Ben. He's nineteen and ridiculously tall. Me still being only 5ft 2in made it quite difficult when I went to kiss him but luckily I was wearing heels. He's been texting me and wants to take me out for dinner this week. It's exciting but at the same time I don't know if I'm just going along with it because I want someone to like me. Every week when I go out I search for people who will give me attention; any guy who's looking my way I'm happy to go and snog in a corner.

It seems that all those positive feelings I had when I came back from Madagascar have just leaked away with the start of sixth form. Criticisms from other people make me feel bad about myself again, and I want to hide away from both them and myself. It makes me feel awful to think about it now, but at the time I'm usually so drunk that I don't actually care. It's just nice to get some attention, particularly from an attractive guy, and to feel loved. Drinking helps as well because it makes you forget about how you feel; it makes me forget that I feel fat and short and that I'm actually only sixteen and shouldn't even be drinking in the first place. It means I can just go out and have a good time with my friends and not be worried. It's just that when I crawl into the house early in the morning I remember Mum's in bed alone, and it comes back to me that all she wants is some love and attention, too.

3 OCTOBER 2004

I can now say that for two weeks I was officially not single. Ben took me out for a meal to La Scala in Beverley and we started seeing each other pretty much straight away. For the first week or so it was really good (Mum even talked about taking me to the family planning clinic because he was so old!), and I was so proud of the fact that I actually had a proper, serious boyfriend. Then, all of a sudden, I realised that that was all it was; I was just with him because I wanted a boyfriend. He's such a lovely guy but I didn't fancy him and definitely didn't want to be with him. I called him yesterday and told him I didn't want to be with him any more and so here I am, back to square one, thoroughly single and completely alone.

Mum, on the other hand, may be going in the opposite direction. A couple of nights ago she got extremely hysterical. I think everything had just come to a head for her, and seeing me going out and meeting new people had renewed her fear that she was going to grow old alone. After consoling her for what seemed like hours, I mentioned that perhaps she needed someone else to talk to, like a grief counsellor or a support group. I even told her about last year when, a couple of months after Dad had died, I joined a bereavement group online. It had helped me to talk to other people about what was going on in my head without having to disturb and upset Mum. The idea of talking to someone else seemed to appeal to her, and the idea of that being online seemed even more of a good idea. Yet somehow I think she got the wrong end of the stick. Yesterday she joined a couple of internet dating sites. It's very, very worrying.

28 OCTOBER 2004

Oh my God, it's actually happened! I've had the best week ever!

It started last weekend. It was Emma's seventeenth birthday and Abby, Jess, Helen and I had all decided it would be great to throw her a surprise party. Her mum was involved as well, and so the party was held at her house. It was similar to my going away party, but this time there were lots of people from sixth form there. Also knew that a boy who apparently quite liked me was going so I was very much excited. Anyway, this time I was determined not to get so drunk that I would embarrass myself.

It started out really well. I was getting on with some of the boys from my year and was even flirting a little bit with Charlie – that's the guy from my history class that I've heard likes me. I was having a really good time, just chatting to some friends and playing giant garden jenga, when someone tapped me on the shoulder. It was Mark. Although he is in the sixth form with me he's in the year above and the two years are never on the same site, so I haven't seen him for a while. I really thought I'd stopped liking him and that I could maybe have forgotten about the last time I'd seen him properly, but when I turned round and saw it was him all my old feelings came rushing back. He looked gorgeous (as usual) and I couldn't hold down the butterflies in my stomach. I knew that after the way he had treated me last time I shouldn't have even bothered with him but I couldn't help myself. He asked me if we could go and talk inside. He apologised for what had happened at my going away party and explained that since I'd come back he had realised that maybe he'd made a mistake telling me he didn't want to be anything more than friends. I totally could not believe what I was hearing. Emma walked past, overheard our conversation and pulled Mark to the side. She knew how much he had hurt me last time and warned him that if he did anything to hurt me again she would personally castrate him in public. God, how lucky I am to have a friend like her!

But I knew what I wanted and I dragged him through into the lounge where we sat on the sofa and kissed each other. It was totally unbelievable. For the first time in ages I felt like someone was actually kissing me for a reason and not because I was drunk and throwing myself at them.

We kissed on the settee for the remainder of the night and even when Emma's mum came in and saw us wrapped up in an embrace I wasn't embarrassed. And the best thing was, I was fairly sober!

A couple of days later, on Wednesday, he came round to my house. We just sat and talked for ages and I felt so comfortable with him. It just seems right! When he left I asked what was going on between us and whether or not I could tell people we were boyfriend and girlfriend. He asked whether I wanted to tell people he was my boyfriend. I answered in the affirmative – that was, if it was what he wanted. Luckily for me it was, and now here I am, finally in a proper relationship! Arrrgh! I'm so excited!

This weekend I get to go round to his house and we are going to have our first night out as a proper couple. All the usual things are, of course, going through my head, number one obviously being what the hell am I going to wear? I'm also worried about meeting his friends and his family. God, I hope they like me.

Mum's had developments in her life, too. She has met a few people online and has been exchanging emails and phone calls with a couple of them. It's all very new and exciting to her, but I can't help feeling cautious about it. What if, in her loneliness, she gets carried away and moves too quickly? I can't bear the thought of her being hurt again. Even though I was the one to suggest talking to people online there's no way I think she's ready for the kind of relationships other people want on those dating sites. I worry about her so much, more than I think she knows. Everything I do I consider the impact it has on Mum. I'm even conscious about what's happening between me and Mark, just in case me starting a new relationship upsets her.

Part of me thinks that it shouldn't be like this. I shouldn't have to spend twenty-four hours of my day being concerned about her, but then again I guess it's no different from when our lives used to revolve around Dad. The point is that I'm never going to stop worrying about Mum just as I'll never stop being concerned about my sisters. Even if she does end up getting together with someone else in a few years, even remarrying, I'm always gonna fret over her. Sometimes I just wish I didn't worry and analyse so much. It would make life so much easier if none of us really gave a shit about each other!

13 NOVEMBER 2004

I've just got home. Very exhausted. Have spent the last five days on a school history trip to Berlin, visiting war graves, mass cemeteries, museums and prison camps. The whole experience was fascinating yet devastating and harrowing all at the same time. In each place we went to the hush of death was consuming. We would file off the coach, a noisy, rowdy group of sixth-formers, and be instantly silenced by row after row of small white crosses and millions of poppies. With every memorial we visited I felt so insignificant that I actually shrank. When you see death on such a large and horrible scale how can you ever think that anything in your own life matches it in importance? It just doesn't, it's impossible.

I often think I'm hard done by in experiencing three deaths within a month. What about when you're lying in hiding, or waiting in a ghetto as people around you are killed every single day? Just the sheer scale of death in the Second World War is incomprehensible to me. After a couple of days the graves blended in with the scenery. I found it so difficult to actually imagine that number of people dying that I was almost numb to feeling any kind of empathy.

But then, towards the end of the trip, we visited Sachsenhausen, a concentration camp built in 1936. The majority of the outer concrete wall still remains, as do the guards' watch towers, and it is all still covered in barbed wire. We entered through the main gate, a black iron construction which bears the slogan *'Arbeit Macht Frei'* ('Work Makes You Free'). Just the building itself was so utterly terrifying I couldn't imagine what the place would have been like with SS guards and thousands of prisoners. The majority of the prisoner barracks were no longer standing but there were a couple that remained, which had been turned into a small museum housing some of the artefacts that had been found after the war was over. Staring at the photographs and the stained, striped overalls of a prisoner, I began to be able to put faces to the gravestones I'd seen earlier in the week. There were diaries that were not dissimilar in appearance to this one. It really brought it home to me there and then that these were just ordinary people who suffered a slow and horrible death.

On the way back to the coach we were shown by our guide the way in which the barracks were set up. The semi-circle shape faced the gate house and each separate block was aligned perfectly so there were precise rows in between each. This was so the guard on duty could see any prisoner standing in any one of these rows at any one time and have the perfect shot to kill him. Horrible. We were also taken to the remains of one section of the camp which was used for torture and interrogation. The walls had nearly all gone but in the middle of the ruins stood a long metal pole with various hooks and twists. It was here, our guide told us, that prisoners were hung up in such a way that their internal organs would be under too much strain and the prisoner would eventually bleed to death. At this point a girl in the upper sixth collapsed on the ground in front of me. It was all just too much to deal with.

We also saw the remains of the gas chambers and walked the path that would have been taken to remove the bodies and burn them in the huge brick ovens. When we got back to the coach there was complete silence until we returned to the hotel. I don't imagine anyone could stop thinking about it.

That night, after my roommates had gone to bed, I couldn't sleep. My thoughts were still haunted by the images of our day. I tiptoed into the corridor and crouched down against a nook in the wall. It was late and I knew there wouldn't be anyone around. It was there, curled up in a little ball, that I cried solidly and hysterically. Even now we're back home I'm not entirely sure what I was crying about that night; perhaps the things I had learned or experienced on the trip, or perhaps for more personal reasons. All I know is that I felt so stupid and so shallow. The whole trip made me realise that things like this, on this huge horrific scale, happen all the time. Wars are going on as I write, people are dying horrible deaths, and I'm still obsessed and saturated with my own grief and have been for over a year. I know I have a right to miss Dad but I really have to accept the fact that shit happens and that I must deal with what's going on in my life right now and the future that I am lucky to have in front of me.

2 DECEMBER 2004

M um and I had a chat tonight about how serious things are getting between me and Mark. It was pretty embarrassing for me but I noticed as we were talking that she had a tear in her eye. I asked her what was wrong and she started gently sobbing. It turned out that she'd actually been giving the whole situation a lot of thought and without Dad here to consult she was worried she wasn't doing the right thing by me. She explained that, in the case of each of my sisters when they were getting together with their first boy-friends, she and Dad had sat down with them together and talked about the best option. It sounds pretty cringe-worthy (and very Brady-esque!) but that was always what happened. Every time there was an important decision to be made they made it together. Yet here was Mum, all on her own, worrying that she wasn't bringing me up right.

I haven't really thought about Dad properly in

weeks. I've been too preoccupied with all the changes and excitement going on in my life. Yet Mum mentioning him made me think about what Dad would have made of Mark. He probably would have taken the mick out of him quite a lot, for the fact that he takes nearly as long to get ready as I do and is what my sisters call a 'pretty boy'. He would have definitely have interrogated him well and truly about his 'intentions' for his baby girl. When I was younger and the other three used to bring boys home 'for tea', Dad used to test them with a game called 'My Granny'. It was basically a description of a hypothetical Granny and her likes and dislikes; anything with a double letter in it was favourable. For example, she loves apples but hates grapes, adores butter but detests margarine. He would judge these teenage boys on how quick they were to get the joke; the majority of them never even understood it!

Mum and I finished our conversation by deciding that, just in case I felt I was ready, we would go to the family planning clinic together and get the pill. Although Mark and I have talked about it, I'm not really sure when it will happen. Three of the girls in my group of friends at school have all had sex with their boyfriends already and I'm worried that I'm going to be the last one. I don't want to rush it but I do want to be with Mark when it happens. Somehow it feels like I should be ready now. Mum and I are going to the clinic on Monday; maybe it will be soon after that?

7 DECEMBER 2004

Well, it has happened! Only ten days before my seventeenth birthday. Last night I had sex for the first time. How do I describe my first sexual experience? Well, in a word, painful. It was also awkward, embarrassing and funny. It was all of those negative things but it was so good at the same time. I hate to say it but this morning I felt a great sense of relief that it was actually over and out of the way. I'm glad that I've done it and I no longer have to feel like an outcast whenever the topic comes up at school.

I was so worried before it happened, though, because I've heard so many horror stories from people at school about masses of blood, immense pain and a sense of awkwardness and shame afterwards. Thankfully nothing like that happened last night. Mum and I had been to the clinic straight after school (a very embarrassing experience, especially when most of the other girls in the waiting room were several years younger than me). Although the nurse told me it wouldn't be effective straight away without a condom, when Mark came round later on and we had the house to ourselves it just seemed like the perfect opportunity. He was so sweet and kept double-checking that it was what I wanted.

I felt like my room needed to be right before we did anything so I lit some candles and put some music on my CD player. I think it was a mixture of Motown and R&B but it definitely helped relax us both, especially Marvin Gaye's 'Let's Get It On'. That made me giggle, and then I couldn't stop laughing.

We started out by just kissing and messing around on my bed. Then slowly we started getting undressed and that's when the nerves hit. I was embarrassed about my body and what he would think of it. Would he still find me attractive once he had seen every little bit of me naked? But I began to feel at ease and all of a sudden we were both naked under the duvet. I looked down at him, and then down at me, and it seems ridiculous but I wanted to laugh. I just couldn't figure out how it was ever going to work. Then there was the whole awkward moment when we had to get up and find a condom. Thank God the nurse at the clinic had given me some!

Mark made me feel comfortable, though, and all the way through kept checking I wasn't in too much pain. It really hurt and, this sounds silly, felt a bit unnatural, like something that's supposed to be good shouldn't hurt that much. Slowly, though, it got better and even started to feel nice, and when it was over, neither of us could stop grinning at each other. Pretty quickly my embarrassment about being naked returned, and I remembered Mum would be back soon, so I jumped out of bed and got dressed. For about an hour afterwards we just sat downstairs and watched TV, cuddling on the sofa. I don't think either of us could quite believe what had happened and that we'd both just had sex for the first time. It was a weird feeling yet we were so comfortable with each other at the same time. I made him leave before Mum got home, though, worried that she'd be able to tell somehow. He texted me when he got back home, saying that he'd just walked all the way home grinning like a Cheshire cat.

Mum got home and barely noticed a thing. As I feared, she has thrown herself head first into the world of online dating. A couple of weeks ago she met a man called Simon and all of a sudden things seemed to have accelerated. She spends all her time either on the phone to him or chatting online if they're not out on a date together. I'm finding it very hard to deal with. Not only have I never seen her with anyone but Dad, but I've never considered it a serious possibility. Now she returns home like a lovesick puppy. It sounds awful to say it but I hate seeing her this way because it makes me think she's forgotten about Dad already. After twenty-five years of marriage I didn't think it could be possible but still I fear that it's going to happen.

Today at school was weird. I only told a few of my friends about what happened last night because I didn't want people thinking badly about me. After all, it's not as if Mark and I have been together for that long. I didn't know if I was supposed to feel any different. I mean, people say that when you have sex for the first time you feel older. But I didn't feel any different. I suppose I haven't felt like a child in a long time.

I wish I still was a kid, though. Everything seemed so much easier. I don't know why people my age are in such a rush to grow up; I can't see much attraction in being an adult, apart from the alcohol, but that's proving to be more of a negative thing for me at the minute. Adulthood to me means responsibility, mortgages, debt, worry and getting even older (which just starts off a depressing cycle of worry in itself!). I see girls in year seven or eight at school wearing a full face of make-up or chatting to guys in town and it just depresses me. They should mess about and be innocent while they have the chance, because the way I see it, the older you get the more confused everything seems to become. When I was younger everything was so obvious and easy and I always thought that when I was older I would quickly make sense of the world, that it would become even more black and white. Instead it gets greyer and more blurred by the day.

17 DECEMBER 2004

Today I turned seventeen and I've just got back from my first driving lesson. I'm going with Helen who taught Emma and Rachel. She's really nice but the whole experience is so terrifying I don't think I'm ever going to get the hang of it. We started out on a road just near my house. We talked over a little bit of theory first and then she let me get into the driver's seat. I'm sorry to report that I'm still only 5ft 2in and so had to bring my chair all the way forward in order to see over the steering wheel. My legs were shaking to such an extent that I thought I was going to press the wrong pedal by mistake. The speed limit was 30 miles per hour but I didn't dare go any faster than about 20. Every time a car went past I was so terrified that I either wanted to stop the car completely or just stop concentrating so hard and scream! I felt so out of control.

I'm not even sure if I want to learn to drive now because it's so scary. I've got another ten lessons booked, though, and Mum's agreed to pay for most of them because she feels guilty that she won't agree to take me out herself. It was Dad who helped the other three with their driving lessons, although they often came to blows, and Emma almost ran him over by accident during one session. (He was outside the car, moving around to the driver's side where Emma was sitting, when the car rolled back.)

Mum couldn't ever pluck up the courage to take us, and she feared she would do us more harm than good by being so nervous. Dad was a bit too extreme in the other direction, though. Driving was one of his passions and he couldn't understand why my sisters seemed to be making it so difficult. I can see myself now why they always used to have arguments in the car; it would have been a nightmare!

As it is, Mum's even worse now that I'm driving than she was when the others were learning. Since Dad died she's been a bit anal about safety and about us protecting ourselves. It seems all our nerves have been sharpened and if any of us are more than an arm's length away from each other it has to be in the safest circumstances. Mum's already been talking about getting me a brand-new car. Last year we got rid of the old Ford Fiesta because Mum feared it wasn't safe enough and we got a new Nissan Micra. Kathryn and Rachel have since bought their own cars with the money we were given from Dad's life insurance, and Emma then bought the Micra from Mum. Now it comes to my turn to be looking for a car and she's not happy about me wanting a cheap old banger that I can just drive into the ground. She wants me to get a new one with all the latest safety features. I can see where she's coming from but sometimes I think her fears overrule her common sense. In any case, the way I'm going with my driving I won't even need a car, because it's not looking likely that I'll ever pass my test.

Last Friday was the first time I went round town properly. Mark and I started out in the Queen's Arms, then moved on to the Fox and Hounds and the Hog's Head. It's funny, but when I'm with him I don't feel the need to get ridiculously drunk because he makes me feel confident in myself and I'm not out looking for someone else to prove to me that I'm not worthless. I guess before, when I wasn't with him, that every time I went out it was like a test. I had to prove to myself and to everyone else that I was out with that I wasn't ugly and short and a horrible person. If someone wanted to be with me by the end of the night it was as if I had succeeded in proving that I was attractive, that I was wanted.

BOXING DAY 2004

Well, there's a black sack full of Christmas wrapping paper by the back door, twinkling lights on an evergreen tree and we've just eaten turkey sandwiches for the second time in two days. Everything around me is telling me that Christmas Day has been and gone. Yet in my heart I feel as though I'm going to be waiting for Christmas to come around for ever – that is, Christmas Day the way I remember it.

Until last year and Barbados, the Christmas routine had been the same whenever we were at home for Christmas. On Christmas Eve morning Mum would set off early into Beverley to the market to buy fresh vegetables and pick up some last-minute stocking fillers (including the compulsory apple and orange). Kathryn, Emma, Rachel and I would spend the day wrapping our presents and placing them under the tree.

Our tree was a fake one. It slotted together branch by branch, yet, at over ten years old, it was starting to become rather wonky, and several branches were held to the plastic trunk with brown parcel tape. The lights were always white and small because Mum thought coloured ones looked garish and tacky. The decorations themselves were as unique as we were as a family – no department store collections on our tree! The older, cardboard ones with faded religious scenes sat on the bottom branches. Then there were the home-made ones – stockings or snowman created out of felt with an eye or a button missing and tied onto the tree with a loose piece of festive gold thread. Then came the salt dough creations. Whenever we were bored when we were younger Mum used to make salt dough or play-dough and sit us at the kitchen table to create our masterpieces. After you'd shaped them (into a Santa hat or perhaps a Christmas pudding) Mum would place them carefully on a tray in the oven to harden. They would come out slightly cracked and looking a bit worse for wear but it was nothing some brightly coloured poster paint couldn't sort out. We looped ribbon around the top and hung them from the sturdier branches. These decorations tended to have a one-year life expectancy, though, and new ones had to be made, especially when we found mice in the attic had chewed through the salt dough and that several snowmen were without limbs. Scattered throughout the tree were donated decorations, either from Grandma and Grandad, or Gran and Gramps, or a bauble Mum occasionally got as a Christmas gift from a pupil at school. But the best decorations, which featured near the top of the tree, were ones that we picked up on our various holidays. There was the Caribbean

Santa from St Lucia, the moose from Toronto, the American-football-playing Father Christmas, skiing snowmen from France and the ones from Ottawa that were inscribed with the words 'Griffin Family Christmas'. These were treasured so much that they were put on the tree last, taken off first and always wrapped in tissue paper before going back in the attic. The tree was finished with chocolate decorations and either a silver angel or a wonky star on top.

The house looked beautiful on Christmas Eve, before the arrangement of presents had been destroyed and the stockings were taken down. The table was set, with crackers across each place and name cards sitting between the knife and fork. The whole house was filled with anticipation; it really was special. We even had Christmas cushion covers which went over the old ones for the festive period.

Late on Christmas Eve we'd have a big family meal and then prepare for church. As the other three got older, they began either to work on Christmas Eve or go into town drinking with friends. But usually they managed to meet Dad at the gates to St Mary's. I was probably about twelve the first time I was allowed to go to midnight mass. Before then Mum usually stayed home to peel vegetables or wrap presents while the rest of them were out and I was in bed. When I started to go she would occasionally come, too, but it was always Dad who maintained the tradition. It always seemed really odd to be inside a church with it being so dark and cold outside and with drunken revellers passing every few minutes.

Everyone was wrapped in long coats with scarves, hats and gloves galore. You began to see the same faces every year, Mum and Dad giving nods of recognition to friends or clients. The church was lit only by candles and, with the wreaths and holly decorating the pillars, it was eerie yet so beautiful. The vicar would start by welcoming everyone and then there would be a carol. Mum would sing very loudly, and Dad would sing very deep and out of tune. After the sermon and another carol later we would have a few minutes of silence while the church clock chimed twelve. The vicar then invited us all to wish those sitting around us a very Merry Christmas. This was my favourite bit of the service. Mum and Dad would give you a kiss and a hug and then you'd shake hands with all those around you and wish them season's greetings. It just gave you such a nice warm feeling. I never found it strange that even though I enjoyed this particular service so much I was never bothered about going to church any other time of year and didn't even think I believed in God.

When we got back from the service there would be the tradition of putting up the stockings before we all went to bed. The other three had identical stockings – green, red and white with the words Jingle Bells sewn in. Mine was green and red with white snowflakes. Identical hand-written labels were pinned to the inside, though, and an identical lump of Blu-Tack attached them to the mantelpiece. Then came the rigmarole of putting food and drink out for Father Christmas. This process carried on even after I found out Santa Claus wasn't real at the age of seven (thanks to Kathryn for ruining a childhood dream – sometimes older sisters do not know best!). There would be a carrot for Rudolph, and a glass of sherry and a mince pie for the cheerful man himself. In the morning the sherry had always been drunk, the mince pie eaten and a huge chunk taken out of the carrot. I'm not quite sure why Mum and Dad carried on this charade but it was tradition, I guess, and nice all the same.

Christmas morning always followed the same routine, too. I would wake up first (I think it's compulsory when you're the youngest) and then go and wake everyone else up and drag them downstairs, usually around 7 a.m. While we were investigating our stockings, Mum would wander into the kitchen and put the turkey in the oven before making us all bacon sandwiches for breakfast. Then we'd all sit around the tree and take it in turns to open a present at a time. Missie or Max would be in the midst of all this, tails wagging, knocking several ornaments off the tree, and going crazy at the sight of the wrapping paper.

We'd then prepare for lunch before eating at about 3 p.m. Some years we would have Grandma and Grandad, and later on, after Grandma went, just Grandad, but every year it was a huge affair. Following prawn cocktails and the pulling of crackers, the feast would start. There was the turkey, of course, with Mum's own chestnut stuffing. Then there were pigs in blankets (you know, those tiny sausages wrapped in bacon), parsnips, carrots, peas, mashed potatoes, sprouts, roast potatoes, cranberry sauce, bread sauce, gravy and anything else you could fit on your plate. All washed down with a nice glass of wine or, when we were younger, fizzy grape juice.

The rest of the afternoon passed in a similar way to most people's Christmas Day. We would watch old episodes of comedy programmes on the TV and, later, maybe have a game of Trivial Pursuit, Monopoly or whatever new board game one of us had got that year. At about eight or nine o'clock we'd have turkey sandwiches and then all fall asleep in front of the TV. We were always left with the same feeling – exhausted yet comfortable and satisfied.

It was just ordinary. Lovely but ordinary. You don't think your own family's way of doing Christmas is anything special until it changes. Then every minute of that annual event becomes a distant but precious memory.

Obviously this year was the first one at home since Dad had died. I don't think Barbados really counted as it was so surreal. And, of course, this year we were in a house that Dad had never even set foot in.

We bought a real tree. It's a tiny squat thing, and it's dropping needles at a ridiculous rate, which is making Mum pretty mad. The decorations are the same, except now we have a Barbados Santa and a snowman from Berlin to add to the collection. Our lounge here is square and smaller than the lounge in our Elloughton house. One Venture photograph hangs above the fireplace, the other above the sofa on the opposite wall. Our furniture is the same, as are the books on our shelves, and the family entertainment system still take pride of place in the room.

On Christmas Eve we set off to midnight mass, just the five of us. Mum took mass from the front, as Dad always used to, and this time Kathryn went up to have a blessing, too, almost as if she were trying to cover up the gap. Nick, Kathryn's boyfriend, met us at the church. He'd been out into town, though, and halfway through the service descended into loud snores. It shouldn't have been funny but it really was, and it kept the rest of us from thinking about Dad not being there, while Kathryn did her best to revive him from his heavy slumber.

That night we put up our stockings, just as normal, but I had to remind Mum about the mince pie and glass of sherry. It was a half-hearted effort and purely for my benefit, but she did it all the same. Yesterday, Christmas morning, I was the first awake. It was half past eight, possibly the latest I had ever woken up on Christmas Day. We opened our stockings but Mum had forgotten to put in the apple and the orange so had to rush into the kitchen to fulfil the tradition. It was as if we were trying to get everything just perfect while ignoring the big fat elephant in the room which meant it could never be.

Nick took the role of the male. He was first to get a bacon sandwich, and distracted Missie from the wrapping paper while we opened our presents. Mark bought me some perfume and a teddy bear, really sweet. But as soon as the floor under the tree was empty once more he had to leave and get back to his own house and his own family's Christmas.

Then it was just the five of us once more. We chopped vegetables, listened to Christmas songs, set the table, pulled crackers, drank copious amounts of wine and all got involved in trying to create a festive atmosphere. Then it was time for lunch and as we all sat down at the long table that sixth empty chair was staring at us all. The head of the table was so obviously and glaringly missing. Emma began to cry first. Then she set the rest of us off. To start we were crying because, obviously, he wasn't there and we all missed him so badly. Then we started remembering past Christmases – Dad lighting the Christmas pudding a little too vigorously and burning it, breaking the pressure cooker so the vegetables took all afternoon to cook and not eating till it had gone dark. Soon our tears had turned to smiles; Mum wasn't going to let the day be ruined. The lunch was amazing, as it always is, and not a single dish was missing from the table. Even the special pigs in blankets were there.

After dinner we all flopped in front of the TV. Then, after turkey sandwiches, Mum pulled out some board games she had bought. We played Articulate, splitting up into two teams of two with one person being the judge and timekeeper. It's a word game, so Kathryn and I completely squashed anyone else; if only for the reason that Mum could never get her words out quick enough to describe the action on the card. Either that or she would actually say what the word was and therefore have to choose a new one. One thing about our family is that we're highly competitive and soon it had descended into chaos, with us all shouting that one or the other was cheating, or that me and Kathryn had an 'unfair advantage' somehow. (As if! We were both just amazingly skilled!)

Then it got us talking about playing Scrabble on New Year's Day. Mum's friends Ann and Peter used to invite us round to their house every year for a ridiculously huge meal and to play games. It was always Scrabble, and there was usually a scrabble to claim a place in Dad's team. He would always come out with some really long word that no one had ever heard of using both an X and a Q or two Zs. It often meant taking down a dictionary to find out if he was lying or not. The problem was he was normally right, and usually knew the meaning of it as well. Anyone on Dad's team was guaranteed to win. It was stupid but fun, and a tradition, too. We're not going this year, though, because Mum has booked the five of us into Wood Hall – a huge stately home hotel – for three days over New Year. The other three are bringing their boyfriends, and Mum and I will share a room. I'm a bit upset that Mark won't be there and so won't get to be with him on the stroke of midnight (how much of a ridiculous romantic am I?) but if it means Mum won't be on her own then I'm more than happy with that.

Anyway I'd better go. Tea's ready and I think it's another turkey concoction . . . curry perhaps?

22 MARCH 2005

A m recovering from last night. It was Emma's twenty-first birthday party. Mum hired a room at the new hotel near Willerby, and about eighty or so people came. It was a brilliant night but, like all our family affairs, ended up being fairly emotional.

We had made Emma a huge photoboard with pictures of her from birth to her current age. Mum also wrote a speech, which she delivered just before the cake was cut. I think it was on all of our minds the fact that Dad wasn't there and that the last major party we'd had was for Kathryn's twenty-first, a week before Dad died. It was at that do that Dad had presented her with a cheque for £210 for having never tried a single cigarette. It was a bet he had made with each of us to try and steer us away from smoking, and he had dated it for her twenty-first birthday when she would be in Boston. (It was also nearly three months after he died so she could no longer cash the cheque!) It's almost as if my own efforts to stay away from cigarettes are a waste now. Well, at least I can hope that he knows I haven't (and won't) let him down.

Emma got very upset after Mum's talk, and it was a rather traumatic night for all of us. Especially considering that the guy Mum is seeing was there. He's called Frank. It was odd because Mark was with me and I wasn't used to somebody else seeing the very private side of my family life. To combat any feelings of awkwardness or embarrassment I ended up getting really drunk again. I haven't done it in so long but having Mark there at such a private occasion made me more insecure than ever. We've been arguing a lot recently and I just wanted to forget about everything. At every family occasion Dad seems to be lurking over us like some black cloud and it shouldn't be like that. The alcohol shifts the cloud and makes me feel comfortable again. In the end I was sick in one of the hotel rooms that Mum had booked for the night. Thankfully, I managed to wait until most of the guests had gone home. I don't think Mark was too impressed, though, as it was actually Wayne, who's always there at family occasions, who looked after me. I'm feeling very sheepish and a bit of an idiot today.

I wonder if the situation will be the same at my twenty-first. Will Mum still be thanking Dad for helping create us in her speech? Will it still be so evident and obvious in people's minds? Will I still want to remember him on that momentous occasion and will I still be getting absolutely hammered to deal with my feelings?

25 MARCH 2005

Just got in from school. I shouldn't be home so early but I skipped the rest of my lessons because Mark and I have had another argument; the fourth one this month. He says we argue because I'm paranoid. I think it's more about him not understanding me. I'm his girlfriend, for God's sake, I've got a right to be worried when he spends the amount of time he does with his friends, who are all girls and all beautiful. There's no wonder I get paranoid and self-conscious and think he's cheating on me. I know deep down that a lot of it is to do with my own issues about the way I look, but he doesn't help. He's also just brought up the fact that he doesn't think he wants a girlfriend when he goes to uni in September. That hardly improves the situation, does it? Part of me wonders if I should just put myself out of my misery and finish it before he does. But I don't think I want that, even though we argue so much.

I'm not sure he understands me and what happens at home. When Mum is going on a date with someone he doesn't get why it upsets me; he just thinks I'm not being fair on her. He also doesn't realise that sometimes, when I'm feeling really shit, I just need to cry to make myself feel better, to kind of let it all out. Yet when I do cry he thinks there's something hugely wrong and that I'm just being weird for having a big cry fest! I'm never going to understand the differences between males and females. How can one tiny chromosome make us so completely opposite?

27 MARCH 2005

Today is Easter Sunday. I have to meet Mark later on as he says he wants to go for a walk and that we have to 'talk'. I think I know what's coming. Maybe I should have just finished it a few weeks ago. But at the minute, he's not high up in my thoughts. As I write my diary there is a bag on my bed waiting to be unpacked; it's full of clothes from the last few days. We've just arrived home from a break in the Lake District where we scattered Dad's ashes.

Mum made the decision a few weeks ago that we really needed to do something with Dad's remains, as they were still at the funeral directors following the cremation nearly eighteen months ago. Perhaps she felt that now was the time to do it because she feels more settled in herself and her own life. She's been in a relationship with Frank for a few months now and although he's not a man we would have necessarily wanted her to be with (that excludes everyone but

Dad, of course) they're taking it at a steady pace and she seems more comfortable than I've seen her in months. Maybe she feels that to let go of the ashes would be to let go of Dad and now she's ready to do that. Well, let go of him physically, at least; I know she'll never let go of his memory.

We'd all talked about where we wanted to scatter his ashes but had never really agreed on a place or indeed a time when we could all get together to do it. After another lengthy discussion at the beginning of this month it was decided we should take him to the Lake District. It is a place that holds fond memories for all of us; we had often gone walking there when we were younger, and it's one of the most beautiful, peaceful places on earth.

The five of us arrived on Thursday night. We'd chosen to stay in Windermere because there were loads of walks nearby and we weren't entirely sure where we were going to scatter the ashes. We stayed at a hotel called the Applegarth, just out of the town centre. It was a converted Victorian mansion with open beams and a real fire in the sitting room downstairs. We arrived fairly late (having got considerably lost on the way, as usual) but still managed to get a table in the restaurant. We sat in the conservatory section and, as we all nursed our glasses of wine, contemplated our task.

Mum had always insisted she didn't want Dad to have a gravestone. I don't know if it's because she thought it would be too final; almost as if he could then only be in one place. She also thought there would be a sense of duty in having to go and tend to the graveside, whereas she wanted to feel as though she could talk to him anywhere (and says that she does regularly). I never speak out loud to him, except maybe to sigh to the heavens and curse him for not being here at the times when I need him most.

We collectively felt that we wanted to put him somewhere peaceful with a nice view, a place that was easy to get to so we could come and visit whenever we felt the need. The owner of the hotel became involved in our discussion (after, of course, passing on the compulsory condolences) and offered us the use of some local guidebooks. Throughout this discussion of his future placement, Dad was sitting in a green plastic tub about the size of a small beer keg in the hotel room that Mum and I were sharing. I wondered if he could hear us talking about him. Maybe he was occupying that empty sixth chair at our dining table after all.

After a wine-induced heavy night of sleep, we rose to breakfast at the same table and to make a decision about where to take our green plastic keg. We eventually decided on a walk up to a place just outside the town centre called Orrest Head. At a height of 239 metres it wasn't a challenging trek, but the views across Lake Windermere and the surrounding peaks were supposed to be very beautiful.

The walk started in the comical way typical to most Griffin family ventures. We were all kitted out in our walking gear in preparation for a hearty trek – walking boots, comfy socks, jeans, the lot. Yet we had only walked a few yards from the hotel car park when Mum stopped on a nearby stone wall having decided she needed to change her shoes. Back we went and then started all over again. Several stop-starts later we reached the bottom of the ascent, by which time Kathryn said that carrying Dad was getting too heavy for her and did anyone else fancy holding him while we started the climb? Dad was then thrown (quite literally) through the air as the burden of carrying him was shared out between us. Halfway up there was a little bench where you could stop and admire the view, but there wasn't room for all of us so Rachel simply set down the green plastic tub and sat on Dad! I'm sure he wouldn't have minded.

We carried on, having to walk up a set of stone steps until we reached a kissing gate, beside which lived a miserable-looking donkey and a chestnut-brown horse, seemingly in perfect harmony. Seeing a donkey was so apt, especially when it started making a considerable amount of noise as it saw us drawing close. Whenever Dad had been down we used to refer to him as Eeyore and, for several Christmases and birthdays, we bought him Winnie the Pooh merchandise featuring the gloomy character, so that, during the happier times, he could be reminded that we made light of his illness. The Eeyore business card holder he used to have on his desk was just one of many such presents.

As we made our way through the overgrown brambles it quickly became apparent that we were getting near the top. Due to the time of year a low mist hung around the peak and worked its way around the lower part of the benches scattered around the flat plateau. As we looked out towards the lake our view was slightly obscured by the low-hanging cloud, but because it was getting towards midday the sun was shining through and, after about ten minutes, we had a more or less clear view of the lake and the surrounding seven peaks. It was breathtaking. Although the air was cold, the sun was bright and hot, reflecting off the crystal-blue water. Then, through the clouds, there appeared a small rainbow. It was such a perfect day to do it and such a perfect spot.

There were several other walkers milling around, chatting on benches or playing with their canine companions, so before we could do anything with Dad we had to wait for everyone to disappear. We weren't entirely sure about the laws on scattering ashes in a public place, and we suspected there might have been some kind of permission needed for what we were about to do. As it was, we had nothing but our own sense of what was right, and so Mum thought it was best to wait until the space had cleared and we could perform the task alone. We found a young sapling tree set back from the main viewpoint which seemed an ideal place, as it would be a marker for us to come back to in the future.

Soon enough the area was free from onlookers and we opened the green plastic tub. The lid was simply marked 'GRIFFIN' with black pen. I wasn't sure what we had all expected; I for one had never seen somebody's ashes before. The whole tub was just filled with what looked like a chalky white powder. I couldn't believe it was Dad in there; well, his body, at least. I think I half expected to see some evidence of it being a human body – a bit of ear maybe, or some teeth! Instead it just looked like the chalk dust that lined the floors underneath the blackboards at school. Mum decided to just say a few words, a final goodbye almost, and, after another glance round to check there was still no one watching, we upended the tub and scattered Dad around the tree. But just at that moment the wind picked up, and Dad's remains ended up scattered all over the place. The ground was covered in white specks. The five of us just stood there, looking at our feet.

Then we heard the sound of footsteps and we all looked round. There, instead of a person, was a skinny white dog. He simply looked up at us with big round eyes before proceeding to lick the white powder from the ground. Shocked, we all just gawped at each other, not entirely sure what to do. Then Rachel and I couldn't help giggling, and it was infectious. It was just typical of our family that we couldn't even do this seriously and solemnly. Looking back, it was just how Dad would have wanted it, a little bit funny but very memorable. The dog was quickly followed by his owner and we decided we should probably leave before anyone figured out we were responsible for the person sprinkled over the ground.

The scattering of Gramps's ashes a few months earlier had been a similarly emotional yet hurried affair. Auntie Liz and Gran had gone with others to a spot on the River Tay which he had liked, presumably with another green tub, and sprinkled its contents into the flowing waters. They had toasted his life afterwards with a fitting drink of whisky in a local restaurant.

We each said our own goodbyes to the young tree before slowly meandering back down the path to the hotel. On the way the tub marked 'Griffin' was simply squashed up and placed in the nearest dustbin; it seemed there was no longer a burden to be carried. The plan for the rest of the day was to return to the hotel to pick up our things, grab some lunch and visit Harrogate for some shopping on the way home. After all, what's a ceremony scattering somebody's ashes for if you can't indulge in some retail therapy to make it complete?

We left in a light-hearted but reflective mood. Just like the inquest, it was as if a door had closed. Our task was complete and now we had to move forward; it was another step towards putting the past behind us.

There is a stone column situated at the top of Orrest Head and on it is a Lakeland Guide to each of the peaks you hold in your view. At the bottom is also a quote from author Arthur Wainwright which says: 'That day on Orrest Head changed my life.' Perhaps our day there will have a similar effect on me.

EPILOGUE

It's September 2006. With the summer holidays over and three good A-levels under my belt, I'm sitting (quite proudly) in my room in halls at Leeds University, recovering from the carnage that was last night's student event. I'm studying for a joint honours degree in English and Philosophy. In contrast to when I was sixteen, however, alcohol here is simply an addition to a good night out. I no longer find it necessary to forget about my life and the person I am. At last I feel I don't need to hide away any more.

Looking around my small room, there are snippets everywhere of the person I've become. The photo of my flatmates, Jess, Lisa and Sarah, reminds me of the importance of friends, both new and old. On my desk is the large stack of literary and philosophical volumes that I need for my first term. It seems ironic that part of my course involves analysing and questioning the world when for the last three years I've been trying to stop myself doing just that!

Next to my bed is a photograph of me and my boyfriend of just over a year at my sixth form leavers' ball. Rich is twenty-two and a first-year student at Sheffield where he's studying radiography. He's gorgeous, funny, intelligent and kind. I'm still finding it difficult to believe that I have finally found someone who loves me just for being me, when I'm up or down, drunk or sober, and, most importantly, I think I love him back.

Our year anniversary was spent in Windermere. On the day we arrived I dragged him up the hill to Orrest Head to introduce him to Dad. The donkey and the horse were still there, the best of friends. I nodded my regards to Eeyore while Rich stopped to stroke his friend. It was August and the weather was much better than it had been on that previous visit. The view from the top was superb and the plateau was now scattered with groups of friends having picnics and couples canoodling on one of the many benches. The young sapling had grown into a stronger tree and I knelt down underneath it to examine the small shoots that had sprung up since we had been there last. Obviously there was no sign of Dad's ashes; they had been absorbed into the earth or taken off to distant shores by the wind. I grabbed hold of Rich's hand and simply said: 'Rich, this is my dad. Dad, here is my boyfriend of one year, Rich. I hope you're very pleased to meet each other.' Of course, there was no response. Rich simply leaned into my ear and whispered, 'Am I supposed to say hello?' I knew he wasn't entirely sure what to do in the situation so I eased his anxiousness by laughing at his ridiculous suggestion and we took our place on the nearest bench, blending in with all the other lovers around us. We stayed on top of Orrest Head for about half an hour, just cuddling and talking. Unlike the last time I didn't feel anxious or worried, just completely content and calm. He was at rest now, I could feel it, and for the first time in ages so was I.

My shelves in my small room are scattered with CDs and DVDs, papers and photographs. One of the photos that really stands out is of Mum in a long cream dress holding a bouquet of flowers. It's evidently a wedding picture, yet taken on a digital camera so obviously a recent photo. It always comes as a bit of a surprise to me when I see that the man standing next to her in a tuxedo and with a flower in his buttonhole is not Dad. It was taken on 8 July this year, her second wedding day.

She met Richard online in April of last year, just after we'd scattered Dad's ashes. Within two months of them meeting in person he had proposed. Obviously the shock for all of us was immense, but we could see Mum was happy for the first time in over a year, and that meant more to us than anything else. He loves her unconditionally and adores every single thing she does. Mum cannot believe she has fallen in love again. It was something none of us, her especially, thought would ever happen. It's taken a while to get used to the idea, and I still don't think we're quite there yet. Richard will never be a father to me or any of my sisters, and because he knows and respects that, it makes things a whole lot easier. But the fact that he loves Mum so much means that he does of course have a special place in our lives.

We moved into another new house in December of last year. For me it was a very difficult experience, living with a man I hardly knew, but time was, as ever, a great help, and things slowly became easier. I have at last begun to accept this huge change to my life. Richard has been married before and has two children of his own, one of whom has two adorable children under the age of five, meaning we now have a very large, extended step-family, if that's the correct terminology. This Christmas will see a large expedition to Florida, hopefully to create some new memories; not so we can wipe out the old ones but simply so we can add to the family album of our lives.

I don't think Mum will ever get over losing Dad. The best thing she can do is try to come to terms with the life she has now, and see it almost as a separate life from the one she had before. We worry that because she doesn't talk about Dad any more it means she no longer loves or misses him. Yet she explains that having someone else come into your life and loving them does not mean that your love for others is diminished or even has to be shared. Instead it is time that has to be shared, between the loved ones in your life, and maybe that is more of a problem.

One of the things that has worried Kathryn, Emma, Rachel and me is that Mum will have less time for us. Yet as we all move on I'm sure we would have had less time for her, too, becoming preoccupied with our own new and exciting ventures, and if she had not met Richard, the alternative – her remaining lonely – would have been far worse than having to share her with someone new. She's become almost a completely different person to the mum I had when I was growing up. Her priorities have changed, and that is not to say that they are now right or wrong compared with those she had before. The last three years have simply taught her to take life as it comes and to stop worrying. She is also learning to take the plunge and do things on impulse; last year she started a part-time university course to do her NPQH so she has the qualifications to become a headteacher in the future. She and Richard are planning on slowly travelling the world but for the moment are taking it one half-term holiday at a time.

Next to the photograph of Mum and Richard is the black and white photo of my sisters and I in our bridesmaid dresses on the same day this summer.

Emma's on the end, looking flawless and ridiculously photogenic as always. She qualified as a teacher in June and has just started her first post this month, in charge of a year six class. She still has her bad days, although they're getting fewer and fewer. But then again, who doesn't go through rough times, times of self-doubt and loathing? I know I do. Is she really that different from everyone else simply because she's had the courage stand up and address her problems? She's also just bought her own house, and has gained an independence and confidence that I wouldn't have thought possible a year ago.

Kathryn is next. She's tied up in exams at the minute, which, if she completes and passes them, will mean that in December she will officially become Dr Griffin and have the authority to add about a million letters after her name. She and Nick will move in together in January of next year, all being well. Those two being a couple is one of the only things that hasn't changed over the last three years. Maybe Mum and Dad implanted the idea of a teenage romance too deeply into Kathryn's head. They have been together for nearly seven years now, and when Nick gave Mum away at her wedding this July, I think it was on everyone's minds that perhaps they will be next down the aisle. She has been the one that has had the most difficulty coming to terms with Mum's marriage. I think deep down she still has a lot of grief and feelings of guilt to deal with, feelings that may never go away. But as always, she's still a mother figure to me and very much an idol. I just hope that in the next few years I can achieve half as much as she has. I may not be at Harvard yet but there's still time, Kathryn!

Rachel is last on the photograph with a beaming smile, as usual. She's in her final year at university, having spent her third year in Cornwall working for a major food production company. Over the last year she's grown up, become more confident and really found out who she is. She's been with her boyfriend for three years now and marriage is definitely on the cards for them; that is, marriage, kids, big house, the lot. I haven't come across a couple that love each other more than Rachel and Chris since Dad was alive and he and Mum were together.

I look up at my three sisters and think how proud I am to be related to them. They are three of the strongest and bravest women I know and my best friends. Every day I am reminded that, like having Dad in my life for the time that he was here, I'm lucky they're a part of my daily grind and that I have people like them, because I know there are so many people in life experiencing a loneliness that I cannot begin to comprehend.

In the corner of the noticeboard, tucked behind my timetable and next to some cards and letters, is a large colour photograph. The gold inscription at the bottom reminds me it's an official London Marathon photograph, taken in 1999. The man in the middle is grimacing in pain as he crosses the Embankment, passing the 23-mile mark. He's wearing a green Macmillan Cancer Relief vest and black running shorts. His sports socks are pulled, unfashionably, halfway up to his knee (I'm pretty sure we would have teased him for that on the day), yet you can make out that he has noticed the camera and is partly raising his arms above his head in triumph. Although it's not a particularly good picture I chose this photo of Dad to have in my room because it reminds me that despite the pain, he carried on and finished the race. It reminds me of the struggle he went through every day and that the little daily trials and tribulations I have to deal with are nothing in comparison.

Next to the photo of Dad is pinned a very important letter. It's A4 size and has been folded several times in the past. The illegible scrawl is instantly recognisable to me as is the letter, being written in blue biro on accounts paper and simply addressed to 'The Girls'.

Coming to university has given me the opportunity to be whoever I want to be, to try new things, meet new people and learn not just about the world but about myself. It's difficult coming to a new place and trying to give a short history of yourself in answer to the typical questions asked in Freshers' Week. There's not a day goes by where I don't give Dad a thought, and I have told some people here about him and what we went through as a family. But I don't need to tell others about him to make sure he's remembered. I know I'll never forget him; that would be pretty difficult considering he's there every time I look in a mirror. It's impossible to get away from the fact that I'm half his genetic material and have a lot of his personality traits (probably the bad ones!), but the fact that he was in my life and that I experienced his death has helped to shape the person I am today. I am comfortable in this skin. After years of struggling with secrets, judgements and people's perceptions of me, I finally feel I'm ready to climb the highest mountain and scream from the top that I am who I am, that I'm proud of the person I've become, and guess what? I'm still only 5ft 2in!

My flatmates have arrived in my room, leaping onto my bed, bottle of wine in hand for a chat about tonight's plans. I accept a glass and propose a toast. As I raise my glass, in preparation for tonight's big night out, I toast life, living it to the full and not having any regrets.

Cheers, Daddy.

APPENDIX

If you or your family have been affected by depression there are many organisations and groups that can offer support and assistance. Here is a brief list of some of the groups that may be able to help.

DEPRESSION ALLIANCE

Depression Alliance (DA) provides information, support and understanding to anyone who has been, or is affected by depression. They have produced a series of publications on depression and can provide details of a national network of self-help groups.

Website: www.depressionalliance.org

Tel.: 0845 123 2320 (Monday–Friday; 1 p.m.–5 p.m.)

FELLOWSHIP OF DEPRESSIVES ANONYMOUS

FDA is a UK nationwide self-help organisation made up of individual members and groups that meet locally on a regular basis for mutual support.

Website: www.depressionanon.co.uk

Tel.: 0870 774 4320 (Monday–Sunday; 24 hours a day)

MIND

Mind is the leading mental health charity in England and Wales. They aim to challenge discrimination, influence policy and educate the public about mental health issues, and provide a confidential helpline, publications on a variety of mental health issues, drop-in centres, advocacy, counselling and befriending services.

Website: www.mind.org.uk

Mind*info*line: 0845 766 0163

SAMARITANS

Samaritans are available 24 hours a day to provide confidential emotional support to people who are experiencing feelings of distress or despair.

Website: www.samaritans.org

Tel.: 0845 790 9090 (Monday–Sunday; 24 hours a day)

SURVIVORS OF BEREAVEMENT BY SUICIDE (SOBS)

SOBS provide specialist emotional support and practical information for people bereaved by suicide.

Website: www.uk-sobs.org.uk
Tel.: 0870 241 3337 (Monday–Sunday; 9 a.m.–9 p.m.)

WINSTON'S WISH

Helps bereaved children and young people rebuild their lives after a family death. Winston's Wish offers practical support and guidance to families, professionals and anyone concerned about a grieving child. The website contains a lot of material to support young people and a special adult-free zone.
Website: www.winstonswish.org.uk
Tel.: 0845 20 30 40 5 (Monday–Friday; 9 a.m.–5 p.m.)

YOUNGMINDS

YoungMinds is the national charity committed to improving the mental health of all babies, children and young people up to the age of 25. They provide a Parents Information Service as well as training and consultancy, and publications for young people, parents and professionals covering a range of issues including depression, bullying and self-harm.
Website: www.youngminds.org.uk
Parent Information Service: 0800 018 2138